Foreword

For many, our first taste of long-haul travel would have been on a widebody aircraft, particularly a Boeing 747 or 777, or Airbus A380. For over 50 years, the widebody aircraft has been an iconic symbol in our skies – a wonder of engineering and design.

Originally designed for improved efficiency and passenger comfort, as well as increasing cargo capacity, from their introduction in the 1970s, widebody aircraft have helped democratise international travel, opening up new routes for airlines and shortening flight times between hubs.

Like so many good intentions though, economics prevailed, and airlines quickly realised that more seats meant more revenues, and densification became the norm. Typically, the fuselage diameter of a widebody jet allows for the preferred 2-3-2 configuration for seven passengers abreast in a single class cabin. This is also claimed to be the most optimal seating arrangement, although 3-4-3 (10 passengers abreast) has gained popularity with some operators.

In 2015, Emirates unveiled a new Airbus A380 with 615 seats surpassing the previous record holder, the 538-seat Air France A380. It did so at the expense of removing its famed shower facilities and first-class cabin. More economy seats mean a higher profit-per-seat, especially on high-density routes with leisure passengers.

As engineering, engine and manufacturing processes have improved, the cabin interior on widebodies has too. The competition between Airbus and Boeing, the two dominant forces in the market, has helped create accommodation that has been imaginatively stretched by designers. For instance, Virgin Atlantic's A350 features the Loft, a social lounge space available to passengers flying Upper Class. Etihad has the fabled Residence – a three-room suite on the top deck of the A380 cabin, which offers a personal butler, double bed, and private bathroom with shower among its features. Fellow Middle Eastern airline Qatar Airways offers its revolutionary Qsuite, now in its second iteration, on its 777 and A350 fleets.

However, economics are at play once more. Sales of widebody aircraft have been tapering off for a number of years. Both Boeing and Airbus have begun introducing narrowbody aircraft capable of matching the performance of these widebody giants, but more efficiently and sustainably. Indeed, market conditions have led to the retirement of both the 747 and A380 from production.

But this isn't the start of the demise of the widebody. The introduction of the A350 and the impending introduction of the 777X is ushering in a new and continued era for widebody aircraft, and then there's always the freighter market – a loyal customer of these designs.

As long as we wish to travel, and as long as we want our Valentine's Day roses, or next must-have product, there's a widebody aircraft to suit our needs.

Alex Preston
May, 2025

BELOW • *A Lufthansa A380.*

Contents

72

96

52

ISBN: 978 1 83632 110 1
Editor: Alex Preston
Senior editor, specials: Roger Mortimer
Email: roger.mortimer@keypublishing.com
Cover Design: Steve Donovan
Design: Key Publishing and SJmagic DESIGN SERVICES, India
Advertising Sales Manager: Sam Clark
Email: sam.clark@keypublishing.com
Tel: 01780 755131
Advertising Production: Becky Antoniades
Email: Rebecca.antoniades@keypublishing.com

SUBSCRIPTION/MAIL ORDER
Key Publishing Ltd, PO Box 300, Stamford, Lincs, PE9 1NA
Tel: 01780 480404
Subscriptions email: subs@keypublishing.com
Mail Order email: orders@keypublishing.com
Website: www.keypublishing.com/shop

PUBLISHING
Group CEO and Publisher: Adrian Cox

Published by
Key Publishing Ltd, PO Box 100, Stamford, Lincs, PE9 1XQ
Tel: 01780 755131 **Website:** www.keypublishing.com

PRINTING
Precision Colour Printing Ltd, Haldane,
Halesfield 1, Telford, Shropshire. TF7 4QQ

DISTRIBUTION
Seymour Distribution Ltd, 2 Poultry Avenue, London, EC1A 9PU
Enquiries Line: 02074 294000.

We are unable to guarantee the bona fides of any of our advertisers. Readers are strongly recommended to take their own precautions before parting with any information or item of value, including, but not limited to money, manuscripts, photographs, or personal information in response to any advertisements within this publication.

Welcoming the Widebody

Economics, operational requirements and passenger expectations helped create the conditions for the introduction of the widebody jet era. Tim Guest traces the development.

ABOVE • *The first manufactured 747 at Boeing's Everett factory in 1968, with cabin crew representing all the airlines with orders for the aircraft.* QANTAS

When the first widebody airliner entered service in 1970, it followed a period during which transatlantic, long-haul, and general commercial aviation for both tourism and business travel had grown hugely in popularity. And while the single-aisle stalwarts of the 1960s skies, such as Boeing's 707, were very successful aircraft, they simply could not carry enough passengers to meet the growing appetite for flying their success had helped create, nor the corresponding fresh commercial demands of the major airlines.

The late 1950s and 1960s saw the introduction of several superb, single-aisle aircraft designed to meet the needs of commercial airlines and their passenger-number expectations of the time. Yet, with the success of such single-aisle planes as Boeing's 707, 720 and 727 series, as well as Convairs, Vickers VC-10s, Douglas DC-8 aircraft and others in delivering comfortable, convenient, and evermore affordable short and long-haul travel during those years, the major airlines plying international routes needed more. American, BOAC, Northwest Orient, Pan American, and Trans World all

began looking to a future when a wider-fuselage, twin-aisle plane would enable them to carry many more passengers than the 200 or so people a narrow-body like the 707, currently allowed.

Engineering Genius

Aeronautical engineers had to find ways of solving these growing demands in their new airframe designs, designs that not only had to carry extra passengers, but had to do so with greater operational cost-efficiencies, while flying increasingly greater distances. As a result, existing designs were stretched and expanded, leading to longer, wider, and taller fuselage plans entering the picture. Designs were, however, constrained by the regulations of the time; the idea of having full upper and lower decks to maximise passenger numbers was simply not possible with emergency evacuation requirements as they were in the 1960s. A partial double deck design was, nevertheless, possible and appeared with the first wide-body jet, the iconic Boeing 747 jumbo** in 1970 and, together with its twin aisles, this new design was the first step in aviation's wide-body revolution.

The twin-aisle concept that emerged did so, coincidentally, at a time when air-fare deregulation took place in the US, and while two aisles was the design factor most important in facilitating increased passenger numbers, combined with deregulation

the airlines could now also become more creative with their ticket prices. They could go beyond just the separate coach/economy-class and first-class differentiations that had been introduced in the 1950s. From the first 747 that flew to the subsequent wide bodies of the 1970s and beyond, the airlines could now offer affordable long-haul travel for the masses, such as found in Pan Am's coach-class on its first 747 long-haul flights. But with their new cabin real estate other configurations and different seating, such as wider seats, became possible, creating opportunities for a greater range of onboard services, new fares, and an increased number of revenue streams. Pan Am, again, led the way when it introduced its Clipper-Class

product in 1978, effectively a business-class experience with bespoke menus, improved seating, and leg room; it's fare and revenue stream took its place between coach and first-class. In 1979, Qantas followed suit, though this time introducing a named Business Class fare and service that also featured

___

** While the original jumbo jet was, indeed, Boeing's 747, the term jumbo was adopted in one form or other to describe other wide-body aircraft that eventually emerged during the early to mid-1970s. Latterly, the Airbus A380, for instance, has become known as a super jumbo jet and the Airbus A350-1000, as well as Boeing's 777X, termed mini-jumbo jets.*

ABOVE • *The vibrant 1970s economy-class cabin of the first Qantas Boeing 747.* QANTAS

BELOW • *By October 2020, British Airways had retired its 31 remaining 747s from commercial service as a consequence of the devastating impact the Covid-19 pandemic had on the airline and the aviation sector.* BRITISH AIRWAYS

the engineers had factored into their designs and that related to the uncertain passenger-carrying longevity of these large-capacity, though relatively slow leviathans; there were industry views at the time predicting that passenger flight was heading for a supersonic future that would shorten the lives of these new subsonic giants for that purpose. Industry futurologists saw an eventual reversion to smaller, faster aircraft and, as a result, widebodies were designed from the outset to be equally as adept at cargo and freight carriage as for commercial passenger flight. It made great economic sense as a fall-back for both the aircraft manufacturers and carriers alike. And, in this regard, it was the wider fuselage designs, such as Boeing's 747, the McDonnell Douglas DC-10 and the Lockheed L-1011 Tristar, with as many as 10 seats across their twin aisles, that were the preferred designs for such a purpose. They had sufficient width when converted to a freight-carrying role to carry two standard 8x8 cargo pallets side by side, not to mention the fact that their designs, combined with those widths, made the conversions relatively straightforward.

a wider more comfortable seat with added leg room.

While the two aisles in a wide-body fuselage five, six, or more metres wide met the initial business expectations and aims of carriers with between seven and 10 seats fitted in each row, thereby increasing passenger numbers in some cases close to 500, the greater space allocation and higher levels of comfort offered throughout the new aircraft compared with single-aisle planes was not

to last. When carriers did the math, they decided the initial leg room and cabin space allocated to seating throughout the planes that had delighted early widebody flyers, particularly in the then coach-class sections, could be reduced to make way for even more seats.

The Cargo Factor

There was another consideration impacting the economies of these first widebody planes, though one

And Then There Were...

But while that first Boeing jumbo jet marked the start of the widebody wars, the four-engine, partial double-deck plane was soon joined in the skies by

the trijets of the DC-10 and the Tristar. The latter was flown by the likes of Eastern Airlines in the US, with the first twinjet widebody taking to the skies in 1974 in the form of the Airbus A300 with Air France. Later, during the 1980s and '90s, a steady series of widebody take-offs proceeded with the likes of the Airbus A330 and A340 aircraft and Boeing's 767 and 777 planes. And while these mentions are not exhaustive, with even more recent widebodies having entered service through the '90s and into the 2000s, we're moving away from the 'dawn' of the widebody era on which we're focussing here.

The fact is that widebodies came about because airlines in the 1960s were aware that exponential growth in passenger air travel was coming, having successfully plied the skies of the 1950s and 1960s with their single-aisle planes. And they knew they needed newer, bigger, more efficient airframes to manage that growth and maximise new revenue streams. New designs, however, also had to offer greater cargo-carrying capabilities to help maximise cargo income on passenger flights, which itself would help lower passenger fares, and such capabilities would also attract freight-only carriers for the long-term.

In the first instance, however, following years of close consultation and cooperation between Pan American and Boeing, it was Boeing's 747 jumbo that took the world by storm at the end of the 1960s.

Boeing 747 – the original characteristics

Unveiled in 1969 and flying commercially for the first time in 1970, the Boeing 747 jumbo jet revolutionised commercial passenger flying, with its four-engine, partial-double-deck 'hump' design opening up the skies to long-range, high-volume air travel for the first time. Nicknamed, 'Queen of the Skies', amongst other fond labels, the Boeing 747 was adopted by major full-service airlines from the US to Europe, the Middle East, East Asia, and Australia, and became the flagship aircraft of many.

The plane was several years of planning and design in the making. US carrier, Pan American, following on from its success flying Boeing's single-aisle 707 on short, medium, and long-haul routes from the late 1950s through the 1960s, had approached Boeing in the mid-'60s to design a plane around two and a half times the 707's size. A double-deck version of the 707 would have made the airline really happy, but safety constraints made that configuration impossible at the time, so a high-capacity, twin-aisle design was the plan to help Pan Am face the increasingly crowded skies and airports.

Achieving a Milestone in Aviation History

The design that emerged was the 747 and only following Pan Am's commitment to buy the first 25 of the future aircraft to the tune of $525m

in April 1966, did development of the plane move ahead. The extensive collaboration and cooperation throughout these years between the two companies on the development of this new aircraft was unprecedented and the emergence and existence of the 747 jumbo is almost as much down to Pan American as it is to Boeing. That said, Boeing already had a card up its sleeve when Pan Am first made its approach. It was able to reference work it had recently undertaken to design a cargo plane for the US Department of Defense, plans it was able to bring to bear in the design of the widebody passenger aircraft. With a full second deck not a possibility, a partial upper-deck design was proposed, and the jumbo's 'hump' became the landmark feature of the 747, recognised the world over. The plans also delivered the 747's wider main fuselage, which not only allowed twin aisles with more passenger seating, but also solved the aim of incorporating a much greater cargo-carrying capacity, the latter has been the major reason for the Boeing 747's success and longevity in the airfreight sector, even to this day.

From the time Pan Am placed that order for those first 25 planes in 1966, it took just over two years before the first aircraft was completed in September 1968 at the company's brand-new Everett site, 25 miles north of Seattle, Washington State: an extraordinary accomplishment. Then, on February 9, 1969, the new jumbo,

BELOW • *Flying the flag. A British Airways 747 with the famous Negus livery.* BRITISH AIRWAYS

ABOVE • *A WardAir 747. By 1980, the privately-owned Canadian airline had a fleet of four 747s.*
AIR CANADA

BELOW • *Canadian Airlines International Ltd operated a fleet of four 747s until their retirement in 2004, following the airline's acquisition by Air Canada in 2000.*
AIR CANADA

named the *City of Everett*, took its first test flight from the Paine Field airport near Everett and, for the next 37 years, the 747 remained the highest passenger-carrying-capacity plane in the skies.

However, despite the initial speed to complete the first aircraft, testing in 1969 following the plane's first flight hit some issues and took longer to solve with higher additional costs than anticipated. The problems, including with the Pratt & Whitney JT9D engine, were, nevertheless, eventually solved during more than 1,000 further test flights that year, culminating in US Federal Aviation Administration (FAA) Certification on December 30, 1969. The JT9D became the first high bypass ratio jet engine to power a commercial widebody airliner when it powered Pan American's first flight of its new Boeing 747-100, on January 22, 1970, flying the airline's New York-to-London route.

Flying on a Grand Scale

With its entry into service, flying was transformed by the jumbo inasmuch as more passengers meant lower fares for economy flyers and the additional internal real estate meant new premium cabin sections could be added, for which new fares were also created. And in addition to these changes to the economics of passenger flight, freight economics changed as well as a result of the huge potential to carry cargo far and beyond the needs of those passengers flying onboard and was a major reason why fares for the flying public could be reduced as much as they were.

The cargo-carrying capabilities of the plane were helped, in part, by the location of the 747's cockpit on the upper deck; in freight-only versions this meant the full length of the main deck, which varied between variants, could be filled with cargo. Freight versions of the jumbo eventually came with a lifting nose as standard, such as on the 747-200F and 747-400F, while earlier versions could be converted. This feature made cargo loading a much easier task.

The space created by the iconic partial upper deck 'hump' was used by several of the early 747 adopters to create separate and distinct lounge areas for their first-class passengers. American Airlines, for example, offered its upper deck as a lounge with a bar and piano; Australian carrier, Qantas, kitted out its partial upper deck as a themed Captain Cook Lounge; Pan Am's original interior provided its first-class travellers with a restaurant, while eventual early users of the Boeing 747, including Air India, Japan Airlines and Singapore Airlines all provided upper-deck, first-class lounges.

Fundamentally, the Boeing 747 was designed to be the safest airliner ever made and its record, to date, is testimony that such an accolade holds true. From the very first aircraft, redundancy was built into the airframe's systems that was beyond reproach. Back-up hydraulics would take over if main systems went down, dual control surfaces meant the aircraft could still be flown if any of the surfaces failed and the use of four main, four-wheel, landing-gear bogies not only distributed the aircraft's weight more evenly, but they also enabled the plane to

land, if necessary, on just two opposing bogies. In comparison with other aircraft of the day, everything about the 747 was more – more impressive, more luxurious, more magnificent; it was like an ocean liner in the skies. When looking at the construction of its airframe, impressive is an understatement; the 747 required such materials and quantities as: 66,150kg of high-tensile-strength aluminium, 274km of wiring, 8km of various tubing, and comprised over six million parts, of which half were fasteners of one kind or another. But the result was service level and performance characteristics never before achieved, of which the dedicated Boeing team of designers, engineers, and workforce, alike could be proud. That first 747-100 had a cabin 6.1m wide, a wingspan of

59.6m, and a length of 70.6m. Its range was 9,800km and it could carry 173.3m^3 of underfloor freight. The aircraft's maximum taxi weight was 334,750kg and those first Pratt & Witney JT9D-7As delivered a thrust of 20,925kg enabling the plane, at 35,000ft, to cruise at Mach 0.84 or 895kmh.

A Testament to an Amazing Aircraft

Finally, if more were needed to underline the capabilities and safety of this aircraft, a brief mention is worthy of what a China Airlines 747SP, Flight 006 out of Los Angeles on February 19, 1985, went through en route to Taipei. During a period of clear air turbulence, issues with one engine – it was flying on four P&W JT9D-7As – caused

TOP • *Air Canada 747. From 1971 until 2004, the airline operated the 747-100 and 747-400.* AIR CANADA

ABOVE • *SAS Boeing 747 Combi Magnus Viking LN-RNA, cabin interior with its distinctive 1980s onboard service.* SAS

LEFT • *On 3 June 1970, Air France operated its first 747 flight between Paris and New York.* CLEMENS VASTERS

asymmetrical thrust leading to other extreme effects. Pitching and yawing, the plane eventually lost 30,000 feet in under two and a half minutes having been subjected to Mach 0.88 speeds and repeated extreme g-forces from 4.8g to 5.1g when the crew were frantically trying to pull up on a number of occasions to regain control of the plane. The aircraft suffered near catastrophic damage with both wings permanently bent upwards 2-3in at the wing tips, the left-hand aileron was permanently damaged, and both the LH and RH main landing-gear up-lock assemblies separated from their attachments with the landing-gear doors falling off into the sea. Large sections of the horizontal stabiliser had also been ripped off and the outer elevator was completely gone. That the aircraft landed safely with all this damage once the crew stabilised matters is testament to the punishment a Boeing 747 can sustain while still being able to fly.

It's not surprising then, that for many, the Queen of the Skies was, is and always will be, their favourite passenger aircraft.

ABOVE • *Close-up of the 747 during its testing programme, sitting idle at King County International Airport.* REDLEGSFAN21, FLICKR

RIGHT • *A South African Airways Boeing 747-200. During their operation, the airline counted 28 747s among its fleet.* AERO ICARUS

BELOW • *Virgin Atlantic has had 30 different 747s in its fleet over the years.* AERO ICARUS

Follow the Leader

Boeing's 747 was a hard, widebody act to follow, but followed it was. Tim Guest looks at the race by other makers to get their own widebodies into the air.

From the moment Pan American flew the world's first commercial transatlantic widebody flight with its new Boeing 747-100 jumbo jet, in January 1970, the gloves were off for rival aircraft manufacturers to get their own leviathans into service. And they did. Same time, Boeing didn't sit on its laurels with just that first jumbo variant and before too long, in 1971, it added the 747-200 to its portfolio. Among other improvements, the new plane offered more powerful engines that allowed a greater maximum take-off weight of 378,000kg compared with its predecessor's 333,000kg; it also had a new maximum range of 12,150km compared to the 747-100's 8,560km. In 1976, the skies also welcomed Boeing's 747SP – Special Performance – variant, which the company introduced to compete with the earlier arrivals of the McDonnell Douglas DC-10, which first flew in August 1970, and Lockheed's TriStar, which had its first test flight slightly later, in November 1970. The widebody skies of the 1970s were beginning to get crowded.

The McDonnell Douglas DC-10

McDonnell Douglas had been making passenger airliners since the 1950s when it introduced its DC-10 to the paying passenger, on August 5, 1971, with American Airlines. American Airlines had put out a specification to manufacturers in 1966 for a widebody plane smaller than the expected size of Boeing's offering. The plane was to replace the carrier's Douglas DC-8 on mid- to long-haul domestic, as well as intercontinental routes, but as well as being able to fly into any large airport, American also wanted the bigger jet to be capable of flying into smaller airports unable to handle the larger Boeing plane; this would open up additional routes to their new widebody travellers, with resulting new revenue streams. The airline's first order for 25 aircraft was soon followed by an order for 30 from United Airlines. And much like the thinking behind the 747, as well as meeting the passenger specifications of American, McDonnell Douglas also built the DC-10 with the needs of the freight-handling sector in mind.

BELOW • *American Airlines was the first to fly the DC-10, operating 66 of the type until retiring them in 2000.* FOTONOIR/FLICKR

ABOVE • *The DC-10-15 was extremely well-suited to the atmospheric and environmental condition of Central and South America. Mexicana sold some of its DC-10s to AeroPeru.* FOTONOIR/FLICKR

RIGHT • *JAL operated 20 DC-10-40s, mainly on domestic routes connecting Tokyo with regional cities, as well as short-haul and medium international routes mainly in South-East Asia. They were replaced with Boeing 777s and 767-300s.* FOTONOIR/FLICKR

Among its attributes, the new widebody offered excellent fuel efficiency, relatively low maintenance costs and a twin-aisle, passenger-carrying flexibility, typically of between 255 and 380 travellers in two classes for medium to long-haul domestic flights. On the first tranche for American, however, the initial DC-10-10 cabin layout was slightly roomier with just 206 seats, as opposed to the 222, for example, inside United's first DC-10-10 cabins. Nevertheless, both airlines had similar seating configurations of six seats abreast in first-class and eight abreast in economy.

The plane initially garnered a reputation for improved comfort and

style, with its spacious cabin and noticeably larger windows. Marketing at the time advertised the DC-10 as 'probably the quietest jet' people had ever flown, though many over the years would come to dispute such a claim.

The plane had a recognisable trijet configuration, which became almost as well known to the travelling public as the 747's hump, (though the TriStar, similar to the DC-10, in that regard, was soon to follow). Three latest GE CF6-6 high-bypass turbofan jet engines, derived from military F103 designs, equipped the trijet, two on underwing pylons and a third centrally located on the tail at the base of the vertical stabiliser. Various options of the CF-6 engine were used on different variants of the DC-10, (e.g., DC-10-10, DC-10-10CF (convertible passenger/cargo), DC-10-15, DC-10-30), in the coming years, such as the CF-6-50A on the DC-10-30. Pratt & Whitney's JT9D-20 was then used on DC-10-40s, 42 of which were built between 1973 and 1983 for Northwest Orient Airlines and Japan Airlines, the only two carriers to fly this variant. Northwest was behind the decision to use the more powerful engine, which delivered a maximum take-off weight (MTOW) of 251,815kg, as it wanted commonality and compatibility with the same engine as it used on the Boeing 747s in its fleet.

This DC-10-10 was the first variant. Pitched for transcontinental domestic flying, it had a maximum range of 6,500km; later DC-10-30 and DC-10-40 long-range variants could fly 9,600km and were intended for the long-haul intercontinental market. The series -30 had a smaller cabin allowing greater

LEFT • *After troubled times, DC-10s are still holding their own. Tanker 912 is one of four modified McDonnell Douglas DC-10-30 aircraft operated by 10 Tanker Air Carrier of Albuquerque, NM.* STEVE HARVEY ON UNSPLASH

BELOW • *Air Canada was an early adopter of the Lockheed L-1011.* AIR CANADA

RIGHT • *Finnair was a valued customer of McDonnell Douglas. The airline received its first wide-body aircraft in 1975, two DC-10-30 planes flying between Helsinki and New York, and later between Helsinki and Las Palmas.* CLIPPERARCTIC

BELOW RIGHT • *SWISS took delivery of its first MD-11 in 1991.* FOTONOIR

range and height for intercontinental flights and was used by airlines across the world. The -30 and -40 aircraft also had a third main landing gear leg to support their higher weights, which was due to such changes as longer wingspans and correspondingly bigger fuel tanks. The DC-10-30 long-range variant entered service in 1973 and, with three of the GE CF6-50 engines, had a cruising speed of 982kph.

On the freight side, 27 convertible cargo/passenger transport versions of the DC-10-30, the DC-10-30CF, began shipping in in 1973 for deliveries to Overseas National Airways and Trans International Airlines. An all-cargo version of the DC-10-30 - the DC-10-30AF – was due for Alitalia in 1979 but it was delayed, and it was not until FedEx ordered the plane in the early 1980s that production began in May 1984, completing after 10 of the type were made.

In all, between 1971 and 1988, 446 DC-10s of one variant or another were built. One of the differentiating development facets that must be noted before closing this brief look at such a well-known aircraft, was the fact that

as well as innovation, the plane also incorporated many of the tried and tested narrow-body technologies McDonnell Douglas had already used aboard its DC-8 and DC-9 aircraft. While this technologically cautious approach during a time of huge technological change and improvement in the industry had the perceived advantage of making the development of the plane faster and less expensive than rival airframes, only time would tell if what might seem like 'corner cutting', was such a good idea, after all.

Sadly, that brings us to the closing fact of this section. No mention of the McDonnell Douglas DC-10 would be complete without a brief reference to its safety reputation, something that was damaged quite early in the DC-10's career. Without listing event by event, suffice to say that the DC-10's first decade and beyond saw a series of accidents, a large proportion of which were determined to be due to design and engineering issues with the aircraft itself: cargo door problems, engine mounting issues, for example, led to a series of incidents and accidents, some fatal, which resulted in McDonnell

Douglas' new jet facing huge scrutiny and controversy. These early-year tragedies were unfortunate for a plane that was to eventually go on to become very successful and reliable, including its extensive use with the US military for mid-air refuelling, as well as in the cargo field.

McDonnell's next step

Launched in 1986, the McDonnell Douglas MD-11 is a medium to long range widebody jet airliner, which arose out of the development of the DC-10.

Key features included a choice of new GE CF6-80C2 or PW4000 turbofan engines, a slightly wider wing with winglets, a longer fuselage stretched by 11% to 202ft (61.6m), a 14% increase in MTOW and the use of composite materials.

The MD-11 cockpit included a flat screen glass display, with six interchangeable units and advanced Honeywell VIA computers which eliminated the need for a flight engineer making it a two-crew cockpit.

In total, 200 MD-11 aircraft were manufactured between 1990 to 2001,

ceasing production three years after the 1997 merger with Boeing.

Finnair was the first airline to launch the MD-11, introducing compact seat rows when flying from Helsinki to Tenerife in the Canary Islands, a configuration allowing it to carry 402 passengers. During the course of their service, the seven MD-11s Finnair had in their fleet raked up about 400,000 flight hours. Over time approximately 14m passengers have flown on them. The Finnair fleet's last MD-11, with route code OH-LGG, went on its final flight in February 2010, returning from Delhi, India, to Finland, before the aircraft was converted into a cargo plane in Singapore.

Four years later, KLM operated the very last MD-11 passenger flight. The arrival of KL672 - at Amsterdam Airport Schiphol from Montreal, marked the end of KLM's MD-11 operations worldwide. The aircraft had been in service for 21 years, but as KLM continued its investment in a modern, economical, and sustainable fleet, it found no room for the MD-11. The aircraft had become expensive to maintain with its relatively high fuel consumption. Spare parts were also hard to come by making it unfeasible to maintain stocks.

Launched in 1994 at the Singapore Airshow, the MD-11ER included options for a maximum take-off weight of 630,500lb (286,000kg) and an extra fuel tank of 3,000 US gal (11,000 lit) in the forward cargo hold to offer a range of 7,240nm (13,410km), an increase of 400nm (740km) over the standard passenger variant. Only Garuda Indonesia and World Airways ordered the aircraft for which a limited number were produced.

McDonnell Douglas DC-10 and MD-11 selected specifications

	DC-10	MD-11
Length	55.50m (182ft 1in)	61.62m (202ft 2in)
Height	17.70m (58ft 1in)	17.60m (57ft)
Fuselage width	6m (19ft 8in)	6m (19ft 8in)
Wingspan	47.35m (155ft 4in)	51.66m (169ft 6in)
Passengers (max)	380	410
Cabin Height	2.41m (7ft 11in)	2.41m (7ft 11in)
Cabin Width	5.7m (18ft 8in)	5.71m (18ft 8in)
Cabin Length	55.5m (182ft 1in)	46.51m (152ft 7in)
Engines	3 x GE CF6-50C (3 x 50,800lbf)	3 x PW4460/62 (3 x 62,000lbf) or 3 x GE 80C2D1F (3 x 61,500lbf)
Typical cruise speed	M.082	M.083
Max flight level	42,000ft	43,000ft

Source: McDonnell Douglas

ABOVE • *The busiest route for Continental was served by its DC-10 fleet, a triangle between Houston, Denver, and Los Angeles.* FOTONOIR

BELOW • *Air Afrique's first wide-bodied DC-10-30, named "Libreville", was delivered on 28 February 1973, and replaced the DC-8s on Paris-bound routes.* FOTONOIR

ABOVE • *The L-1011-500 was a popular aircraft for international operators.* AIR CANADA

Lockheed L-1011 TriStar

Hot on the heels of the DC-10, Lockheed's L-1011 TriStar was the third widebody airliner to claim a segment of the fast-growing widebody market. Its design was very similar in appearance to the trijet configuration of the DC-10, though instead of three GE CF6-6 engines the TriStar had three Rolls Royce RB211 engines, two under each wing and the third, like the DC-10, centrally positioned on the tail, though in the case of the new TriStar, not below a vertical stabiliser, but rather the L-1011's 'all-flying tail', its stabilator, which improved the overall control surface effectiveness of the new plane. It's worth noting that whereas McDonnell Douglas had been making passenger jets for years, the L-1011 was Lockheed's first attempt at a passenger jetliner.

And like McDonnell Douglas, the company had also been approached by American Airlines in 1966 with the same specification request for a widebody which set it on the path to develop their TriStar jet. However, while the design of their eventual trijet was almost a dead ringer for the DC-10, American did not pursue it with Lockheed due to a higher cost compared with the McDonnell Douglas aircraft. The higher costs were largely the result of the TriStar programme having experienced delays and budget over-runs during its development, all contributing to its third place in the widebody race and the higher price-tag. Ironically, the reputation it eventually gained as a very safe aircraft might well have been worth waiting for, considering the protracted troubles faced by the cheaper DC-10. During its lifetime, the TriStar was involved in just five fatal accidents, only one of which was due to a problem with the aircraft itself.

The first carrier to adopt the TriStar was Eastern Airlines, which took delivery of the first plane on April 26, 1972. With a capacity to carry up to 400 passengers, the aircraft had an initial maximum range of 7,410km. Among its new technologies, one of the aircraft's most high-profile innovations was its Automatic Flight Control System (AFCS). This was the focus of a four-hour-plus demonstration flight in 1972, during which the new system was put into operation and performed without human intervention from take-off from Palmdale to landing at Dulles, a breakthrough at the time.

In September 1977, a new flight management system (FMS) was certified on the L-1011 by the FAA. This had a number of advanced features designed to reduce crew workload and improve the overall fuel efficiency and performance of the aircraft; features included an advanced autopilot system for which the FAA gave the TriStar the accolade of being the first widebody to be certified for Cat-IIIc auto-landing capabilities, which meant it could land with zero visibility in bad weather. Also incorporated in the L-1011 was a Mach/IAS cruise control system, an automatic Rough Air Mode that detected turbulence and adjusted the engine power-setting accordingly, and a descent mode that calculated the optimum point at which to begin a descent. The plane also had four independent, 3,000psi hydraulic systems, unlike the typical three-system architectures and designs of the time. This added a major extra level of safety/redundancy to the control of the aircraft in the event of hydraulic problems; hydraulics being the lifeblood on which all aircraft control surfaces rely, this was an excellent, reassuring feature.

Delta, TWA, and Cathay Pacific became three of the main TriStar users. But with engine challenges and delays at Rolls Royce in producing a more powerful RB211 variant, longer-range Tristars were late to the party and Lockheed faced losses in its programme to the extent that it failed to become profitable with only 250 aircraft sold, when twice that number were needed to break even. Combined with the competition that the DC-10 continued to exert on the same market segments the TriStar was suited to, Lockheed was forced to end TriStar production as early as 1984. The skies simply were not big enough for two aircraft of virtually the same specifications and capabilities, and the DC-10, despite its issues, had stolen the march on the L-1011.

BELOW • *SAS DC-10-30, Dag Viking SE-DFD.* SAS

Early Widebody Carriers

While a wide range of airlines took delivery of the emerging widebody planes that rolled off production lines during the 1970s and beyond, space precludes mentioning them all, though a notable few are worthy of widebody mentions in relation to some of the jumbos they operated.

BOAC

BOAC - British Overseas Airways Corporation – was a great rival to Pan Am, especially on its North Atlantic route in the 1960s. It joined the widebody revolution with its order for 11 Boeing 747-100s, the first of which was delivered in April 1970. For internal company reasons, the aircraft did not enter service with BOAC until April of the following year. BOAC's successor, British Airways, was created in 1974 and in January 1975, introduced Lockheed Tristars on several European routes. Two further Lockheed TriStar-200 aircraft were ordered in January 1979, followed by six in September, British Airways' final TriStar order. Deliveries took place from March 1980 to May 1981. Meanwhile, May 1979 saw British Airways' first of six long-range TriStar-500 aircraft enter service on its London-to-Abu Dhabi route. As well as adding Tristars to its widebody portfolio, British Airways had not neglected its 747 desires and in May 1975, the Rolls Royce-powered Boeing 747-200 aircraft was launched after British Airways placed an order for four aircraft. In June of 1976, British Airways' first two long-range Boeing 747-236s were delivered and operated non-stop on routes such as London-Los Angeles.

Pan American World Airways

The launch customer for Boeing's 747 in 1970, Pan American's initial order for 25 of the planes in 1966 was the precursor to the delivery of more than 60 of the type's different variants to the airline between 1970 and 1985. The airline's contribution to bringing the whole industry into the jet age cannot be understated, nor can its embracing of the widebody concept. For its procurement of widebody leviathans did not stop with the 747, of which it took delivery of several variants over the years; these included the long-range 747SP, which was able to fly the airline's New York-to-Tokyo route non-stop. Pan Am also added 12 of Lockheed's L-1011 Tristars to its fleet at the start of the 1980s in a similar timeframe to it adding 17 McDonnell Douglas DC-10s to its most popular, as well as long-range routes. Following their arrival on the scene in the late 1970s, Pan Am also embraced the first widebodies off the Airbus production line, ordering 13 Airbus A300s and over 20 of its A310 widebody jetliners, adding them to its inventory from the mid-1980s onwards.

United Airlines

United Airlines' first widebody was Boeing's 747, of which six 747-100s entered commercial service with the airline during the second half of 1970. Its 747s were initially operated on long-haul domestic routes, though later flew longer international routes, as well. Over the course of three decades, the airline eventually received over 70 variants of the 747, particularly the later 747-400,

Lockheed L-1011, L-1011-200 and L-1011-500 specifications

	L-1011	L-1011-100	L-1011-200	L-1011-500
Length	54.17m (177ft 9in)	54.17m (177ft 9in)	54.17m (177ft 9in)	50.05m (164ft 2in)
Height	16.87m (55ft 4in)	16.87m (55ft 4in)	16.87m (55ft 4in)	16.8m (55ft 1in)
Fuselage width	5.97m (19.59ft)	5.97m (19.59ft)	5.97m (19.59ft)	6m (19ft 6in)
Wingspan	47.35m (155ft 4in)	47.35m (155ft 4in)	47.35m (155ft 4in)	50.1m (164ft 4in)
Passengers (max)	400	400	400	330
Cabin Height	2.7m (8ft 10in)	2.7m (8ft 10in)	2.7m (8ft 10in)	2.7m (8ft 10in)
Cabin Width	5.77m (18ft 11in)	5.77m (18ft 11in)	5.77m (18ft 11in)	5.77m (18ft 11in)
Cabin Length	33m (108ft 3in)	33m (108ft 3in)	33m (108ft 3in)	33m (108ft 3in)
Engines	3 x Rolls-Royce Rb211-22 Turbofan (3 x 42,000lbf)	3 x Rolls-Royce Rb211-22 Turbofan (3 x 42,000lbf)	3 x RB211-524B Turbofan (3 x 50,000lbf)	3 x Rolls-Royce RB.211-524B Turbofan (3 x 50,000lbf)
Typical cruise speed	M.078	M.077	M.077	M.079
Max flight level	42,000ft	42,000ft	42,000ft	43,000ft

Source: Lockheed Martin

which made up a large proportion of its 747-inventory. United Airlines retired the last of its Boeing 747-400s on November 7, 2017, following a final flight on its San Francisco to Honolulu route. As with other carriers, however, United's widebody eggs were not all in one basket, as it was also one of the launch customers in 1971, alongside American Airlines, for the McDonnell Douglas DC-10. The airline operated a total of 59 DC-10s over the coming years, of which 48 were original DC-10-10 variant airframes, which were to become one of United's key work-horses on many of its routes.

Continental Airlines

Continental Airlines was one of the three early adopters of Boeing's 747 jumbo jet, along with Pan Am and TWA, using it on its domestic routes. It also placed large orders for the DC-10 and, in June 1972, began its widebody DC-10 service, which was needed to address growing market share and growth in travel overall that had been encouraged by its 747 services. One of its 747 accolades was its award-winning, upper-deck, First-Class lounge, and 'Polynesian Pub' main-deck interior, recognised worldwide. So popular were they that the interior innovation was carried over into the airline's DC-10 fleet until necessary interior seating reconfiguration forced by the 1973 oil crisis meant such luxuries had to make way for extra seating. For a time, from 1978, Continental moth-balled its 747s due to low passenger numbers and used just DC-10s domestically and on international routes, though the airline's 747s eventually returned on its Newark to London/Paris transatlantic route.

Trans World Airlines

Another early adopter of the 747, TWA, ordered many of the Boeing planes at the start of the 1970s, eventually owning more than 30 of the aircraft. This enthusiasm for the jumbo, however, proved problematic, as annual passenger number fluctuations made the aircraft viable for only around five months of the year on long-haul routes, a scenario experienced by others. TWA then added a second widebody to its fleet in the form of Lockheed's L-1011 TriStar, with the aircraft's launch into commercial service in 1972 actually underpinned by orders from TWA and Eastern Airlines. At the end of May 1982, TWA took delivery of its 36th and final TriStar. The airline's third widebody was in its sights after 1978, the year Boeing's 767 arrived on the scene. TWA ordered over 20 of the aircraft and the 767-200 entered commercial operations with the airline in late 1982. Between them, TWA's three widebodies helped it to a peak of operational achievement in the summer of 1988, when its three widebody planes accounted for the carriage of over 50% of all transatlantic passengers between New York and European gateway cities.

BELOW • *United Airlines 747.* CONTRI

The Arrival of Airbus

Many cite the A300 as being the aircraft that turned Airbus into a serious contender to the respective thrones of Boeing and McDonnell Douglas. Michael Doran charts the European airframer's early widebody portfolio.

This is not the story of Airbus, nor of the complicated negotiations and political games that surrounded its birth. That is another story altogether. This is about the three aircraft, the A300, A310 and A340 that propelled Airbus onto the world's aviation stage.

Without these three aircraft there may never have been the A330, A350 and A380 that so many millions are travelling on today. It starts with the A300 and the 1969 Paris Air show.

Airbus A300

The first Airbus aircraft, the A300 was born at the 1969 Paris Air Show, when French transport minister Jean Chamant and German economics minister Karl Schiller officially launched the world's first twin-engine, widebody aircraft.

Construction of the first A300 prototype commenced in September 1969 and in September 1970 Air France signed a letter of intent to purchase six A300s, well before the first prototype had been completed.

Construction of the first A300 took three years, and it was shown to the public for the first time on September 28, 1972. The first flight was on October 28, 1972, with the aircraft spending one hour and 25 minutes in the air after taking off from Toulouse-Blagnac International Airport.

The second prototype had its first flight on February 5, 1973, and in total four aircraft spent close to 1,600 hours in flight testing. The A300s type certification came soon after, firstly from the regulatory authorities of France and Germany on March 15, 1974 and followed by the US Federal Aviation Administration (FAA) on May 23, 1974.

The first Air France A300 commenced commercial service with a Paris to London flight on May 23, 1974, but in the early years only Lufthansa and Air France bought the aircraft. While the flight testing was happening, discussions commenced with South Korea's Korean Air about a longer-range version of the A300.

These discussions bore fruit and in September 1974 Korean Air ordered four, longer range A300B4s, with an option for another. Airbus had identified Asia as a potential market for the A300 and believed the Korean Air sale would start opening doors.

Penetrating the European or Asian market was one thing, but it was vital for Airbus to find a way into the US airline industry if it were to make the A300 a success. To get that started,

ABOVE • *The A300B takes to the skies for its initial flight.* AIRBUS

RIGHT • *A handshake that sealed the deal for Airbus' entry into the US. Eastern Air Lines CEO Frank Borman ordered 23 A300s having been impressed by their fuel economy.* AIRBUS

Airbus took the A300 on a six-week tour around North and South America in September 1973.

Among the airline executives, reporters and pilots that viewed the aircraft was former US astronaut, Frank Borman, then the CEO of Eastern Air Lines. In 1977 Eastern Air Lines leased four A300s to trial, which demonstrated that the Airbus used 30% less fuel than Eastern's Lockheed L1011 Tri-jets.

Eastern Air Lines became the first US A300 customer when it ordered 23 aircraft, and this is seen by many as the point when Airbus became a serious challenger to Boeing and McDonnell Douglas.

The breakthrough in the US market came in 1977 when the FAA changed the restrictions for ETOPS (extended-range twin-engine operations standards). The ETOPS rule governed the way passenger jets could operate over water or remote lands and was a big part of why the Lockheed L1011 Tristar and McDonnell Douglas DC-10 dominated the market. When Airbus was able to prove the higher reliability of the A300, the FAA granted certification for it to fly further from an available airfield than previously allowed for any twin-engine airliner. This opened a whole new market for over water, medium-haul flights and the A300 was the first in line to take advantage.

The A300B4 became the first ETOPS compliant aircraft in 1977 and soon grew in popularity for long haul routes in Asia, the US and Europe. Some of the Asian airlines adopting the A300 were Singapore Airlines, Japan Air System, Indian Airlines, Garuda Indonesia, China Airlines and Malaysia Airlines.

The original A300B1 spawned five further variants: the A300B2, A300B4, A300-600, A300B10, later to become the A310 and the MRTT military tanker/transport and the A300-600ST. The A300-600 lives on as the Airbus Beluga, the super transporter used to ferry A380 assemblies from various factories to the final assembly line in Toulouse.

The final variant, the A300-600R had a maximum capacity of 345 passengers or 247 in a typical three-class layout, a range of 4,050nm (7,500km) and a cruising speed of 450kts (833kph). It had a maximum take-off weight (MTOW) of 378,534lb (171.7 tons) and a choice of two engines, the General Electric CF6-80C2 or the Pratt & Whitney PW4158.

In all there were 561 A300s delivered and in June 2022 around 180 are still in operation. Close to 150 are being used as freighters, including large fleets at FedEx Express and UPS Airlines. Airlines carrying passengers on their A300s are almost solely from Iran, including Iran Airtour Airlines, IranAir, Mahan Air, Meraj Air and Qeshm Airlines.

The platform was stretched to make the A330 and A340, shrunk for the A310 and modified into offshoots like the Beluga Super Transporter. The real legacy of the A300 is that it gave Airbus its start in designing, selling, and supporting airliners in extremely competitive and demanding markets.

The A310

During the development of the A300, Airbus also found significant demand for a smaller widebody aircraft, specifically from operators who did not generate enough passenger demand to fill the larger A300.

In 1978 at the Hanover Air Show in Germany, Airbus exhibited a model of the proposed A310, a 28ft 8in (6.95m) shorter version of the A300 with a capacity for 245 in economy or 220 in a two-class layout.

The differences to the A300 were kept to a minimum and apart from the shortened fuselage, the A310, initially called the A300B10, had a smaller vertical fin and a redesigned wing, made by British Aerospace.

The development of the A310 was heavily influenced by launch customers Swissair and Lufthansa, who both placed initial orders for ten aircraft when the aircraft was officially launched in July 1978.

While the A300 struggled with early orders, the A310 got off to a flying start, well before it even had its first flight. Air France and Spain's Iberia Airlines followed Swissair and Lufthansa with orders, with the first UK order coming from Laker Airways for ten A310s.

In April 1979, still before the first flight, Lufthansa raised its order to 25 aircraft with 25 options and two days later KLM Royal Dutch Airlines ordered ten aircraft plus ten options. In July 1979 Air France raised its order from four to 35 aircraft and other airlines ordering the A310 included Martinair, Sabena and Air Afrique.

In April 1982, the first prototype operated the A310's maiden flight and the aircraft obtained its type

ABOVE • *Azerbaijan Airlines was the last airline to operate the A340-500, from Baku to Domodedovo, before its retirement in 2021.* METEB ALI

RIGHT • *The A340-300, with its 283-passenger capacity, has been part of the Lufthansa fleet since the early 1990s. The German airline also operates the newer, ultralong A340-600, which has room for 297 passengers.* AIRBUS

BELOW • *The Airbus A340 Flight Lab's first take-off equipped with outer wing sections designed for exceptionally smooth airflow over their surfaces, as part of EU-sponsored Clean Sky "Blade" project. Known as natural laminar flow, such smoothed passage of air creates less drag than the airflow on traditional wings, potentially reducing fuel burn.* AIRBUS - MASTER FILMS - HERVÉ GOUSSÉ

certification in March 1983. By the time it operated its first flight the A310 had gathered combined orders and options for 181 aircraft from 15 airlines. It entered service first with Swissair in April 1983 as the A310-200.

The -200 has a range of 3,500nm (6,500km), a cruising speed of 459kts and an MTOW of 317,466lb (144 tons). It had a two-person flight crew with a glass cockpit and had the same two engine choices as on the A300.

In 1985 the A310-300 had its first flight and entered service, again with Swissair, in 1986. The -300 had an increased MTOW of 361,558lb (164 tons) and an increased range of 5,150nm (9,540km). The extra range was achieved using additional centre and horizontal-stabiliser fuel tanks, with a computerised fuel distribution system whIch allows the aircraft to be trimmed in flight.

This model also introduced wing tip fences, or winglets, which reduced vortex drag and thus improved cruise

ABOVE • *A Swiss Air A340.*
SWISS

A300 family technical specifications

	A300B1	A300B2	A300B4	A300-600	A300-600R
Length	51m (167ft 4in)	53.61m (175ft 11in)	53.61m (175ft 11in)	54.10m (177ft 6in)	54.08m (177ft 5in)
Height	16.67m (54ft 8in)	16.67m (54ft 8in)	16.67m (54ft 8in)	16.5m (54ft 2in)	16.66m (54ft 8in)
Fuselage width	5.6m (18ft 4in)	5.4m (17ft 9in)	5.4m (17ft 9in)	5.64m (18ft 6in)	5.64m (18ft 6in)
Wingspan	44.83m (147ft 1in)	44.83m (147ft 1in)	44.83m (147ft 1in)	44.84m (147ft 1in)	44.84m (147ft 1in)
Passengers (max)	300	269	269	266	345
Cabin length	36m (118ft 1in)	40.7m (133ft 6in)	40.7m (133ft 6in)	40.7m (133ft 6in)	N/A
Max cabin width	5.13m (16ft 10in)	5.13m (16ft 10in)	5.13m (16ft 10in)	5.28m (17ft 4in)	5.28m (17ft 4in)
Cabin height	2.48m (8ft 2in)	2.48m (8ft 2in)	2.48m (8ft 2in)	N/A	N/A
Max take-off weight	132 tonnes (291,007lb)	142 tonnes (313,053lb)	165 tonnes (363,759lb)	165 tonnes (363,759lb)	171 tonnes (378,534lb)
Max landing weight	122 tonnes (268,961lb)	130 tonnes (286,598lb)	136 tonnes (299,826lb)	138 tonnes (304,235lb)	140 tonnes (304,235lb)
Max fuel capacity	N/A	43,998 lit (11,623 US gal)	62,005 lit (16,380 US gal)	68,137 lit (18,000 US gal)	68,150 lit (18,003 US gal)
Engines	2x GE CF6-50A Turbofan (2 x 49,000lbf)	2x General Electric CF6, JT9D-7Q Turbofan (2 x 53,000lbf)	2x JT9D-59A, CF6-50C2 Turbofan (2 x 53,00lbf)	2x Pratt & Whitney PW4000 Turbofan (2 x 99,040lbf)	2 x CF6-80C2 or PW4158 (2 x 56,000lbf)
Typical cruise speed	M.052	M.074	M.074	M.073	M.082
Max flight level	35,000ft	35,000ft	35,000ft	40,000ft	40,000ft

Source: Airbus

BELOW • *Air France had a total of 28 A300s in its fleet up to 2000, a mix of the B2 and B4 varieties.*
AIRBUS

fuel consumption by more than 1.5%. It had a new two-person cockpit with an array of six CRT displays in place of the traditional analogue dials and instrumentation.

Because it was the same cockpit as the A300-600 pilots could cross-qualify on both aircraft with minimal training under a common type rating. This concept of commonality lives on at Airbus with the A330 and A350.

The A310-300 had more range than any A330 variant and was a favourite for airlines on transatlantic routes. It was marketed to airlines in developing countries as an entry into widebody operations and competed with the Boeing 767-200, which had a similar range.

Sales of the A310 dived when Airbus introduced the A330 in 1994, in fact no sales were recorded at all in the late 1990s, and the last A310 was delivered in June 1998. A total of 255 A310s were delivered between 1983 and 1998 and its place in the Airbus range was taken by the A330-200.

As of April 2025, there are still around 12 active A310-300 aircraft operating commercially, with five in military

service. The main commercial operator is Iran Airtour, followed by Ariana Afghan Airlines, and Yazd Airways.

An interesting legacy from the A300/A310 era is the A310 MRT/MRTT. The Airbus A310 MRTT is a military in-flight refuelling tanker transport and is a development from the A310 MRT multi-role transport aircraft.

Both the MRT and the MRTT are specialist military conversions of the civilian A310-300C wide-bodied

passenger jet. However, just as with the passenger aircraft, the A330 took over this space as well with the aircraft now based on the A330 platform and known as the A330 MRTT.

The A310 was another crucial step for Airbus as it built its widebody reputation and business. As technology and airline demands changed, Airbus had to pivot again, this time to the A340.

Airbus A340

The A300 aircraft got Airbus going and in its preparation for that programme it studied what other derivatives it could build to broaden out its product offering. Airbus had decided to compete head-on with Boeing and McDonnell Douglas with an aircraft for each market.

From its studies, Airbus focussed on two complementary aircraft concepts - the A300B11 and the A300B9. The B11 was a quad-jet that would seat between 180 and 200 passengers with a range of 6,000nm (11,000km). It was seen as a replacement for the aging and less-efficient Boeing 707s and Douglas DC-8s still operating.

The B9 was a stretched A300 twin-engine jet that offered the same payload and range of a DC-10 but used between 25% to 30% less fuel. It was aimed at high-capacity, medium range routes to replace the Lockheed L-1011 Tristar and the DC-10.

The programmes were renamed as (Twin Aisle) TA9 and TA11, which would share the same wing and airframe to save development costs. The first specifications for the two aircraft were released in 1982, with the TA9's range set at 3,300nm (6,100km) and the TA11s at 6,830nm (12,650km).

In January 1986, Airbus announced the TA9 was to be the A330 and the TA11 the A340 and that it

The first flight of the A340 was on October 21, 1991, followed by 2,000 hours of flight testing using six aircraft. After a year of testing and development, European certification was granted on December 22, 1992, with the FAA following in May 1993.

The first A340 was delivered to Lufthansa in February 1993 and was to replace its aging DC-10s on the Frankfurt-New York route. Air France received its first A340 in the same month and used it replace a Boeing 747 on its Paris-Washington DC service.

Nonstop services from Europe to Australia have recently hit the news again with Australia's Qantas ordering Airbus A350s to operate a direct Sydney to London or New York service. However, nearly 30 years ago in 1993,

ABOVE LEFT • *SAS Scandinavian Airlines A340 cockpit. In 2020, SAS officially retired its last A340. The A340-300 flew from Copenhagen to Tucson, Arizona in the US before heading to its final home at Pinal Airpark, Arizona.* SAS SCANDINAVIAN AIRLINES

ABOVE RIGHT• *In November 2021, High Fly landed a A340-313HGW (High Gross Weight) on an Antarctic blue glacial ice runway, having flown five hours from Cape Town, South Africa. It was the first time an A340 has touched down in Antarctica.* MARC BOW/HI FLY

would finalise the specifications with prospective launch customers. The A330 and A340 programmes were jointly launched on June 5, 1987, and by then the orderbook had grown to 130 aircraft from ten customers, of which 89 orders were for the A340.

Airbus partners invested heavily in building new facilities for the A330 and A340 production, including new facilities at BAe in the UK and the construction of a new assembly plant in France at the Toulouse-Blagnac Airport, where Airbus stands today.

RIGHT • *Afghanistan's Kam Air is just one of a handful of airlines still operating the A340. It currently has four A340-313s, the only Airbus aircraft in its otherwise Boeing fleet.* ANNA ZVEREVA, FLICKR

BELOW • *SWISS flies its fleet of five A340s on routes between Zurich and Boston, Johannesburg and Shanghai and Osaka. In 2020, the airline completed a cabin refurbishment of all five.* SWISS

an A340 flew from the Paris Air Show to Auckland, New Zealand in 21:32 hours, was on the ground for five hours and then returned to Paris in 21:46 hours.

The flight broke several world records with the A340 arriving back in Paris 48 hours and 22 minutes after it left. The 10,409nm (19,277km) Paris to Auckland longest flight record stood until 1997, when it was broken by a 777-200ER Seattle to Kuala Lumper flight of 10,823nm (20,044km).

During its life, the A340 was converted into four variants, launching with the A340-200 and A340-300, followed by the A340-500 and the A340-600. The first A340-500 was delivered to Emirates in 2003, who used it to launch its first US service, on the nonstop Dubai to New York route.

The -500 was made for ultra-long-haul flying with a range of 9,000nm (16,670km) in a typical three class layout of 313 passengers. Compared to the A340-200, it has a stretched fuselage, larger vertical tailplane, horizontal stabiliser and wing and significantly more fuel capacity. It could travel nonstop from Perth to London long before the A350 or 787 were built and found a home with many legacy carriers, including Singapore Air, Etihad, Emirates, El Al, Finnair, TAP Air Portugal and Thai International.

The introduction of twin-engine ETOPS opened markets for the A300 and A310 but virtually left the A340 with no market of its own. As engines became more reliable and twin-engine aircraft could fly on almost any

A310 family technical specifications

	A310-200	A310-300
Length	46.66 (153ft 1in)	46.66 (153ft 1in)
Height	15.9m (52ft 2in)	15.86m (52ft 2in)
Fuselage width	5.64m (18ft 6in)	5.6m (18ft 4in)
Wingspan	43.9m (144ft)	43.9m (144ft)
Passengers (max)	280	280
Cabin length	33.25m (109ft 1in)	33.24m (109ft 1in)
Max cabin width	5.28m (17ft 4in)	5.28m (17ft 4in)
Cabin Height	2.33m (7ft 8in)	2.33m (7ft 8in)
Max take-off weight	142 tonnes (313,053lb)	164 tonnes (361,554lb)
Max landing weight	121 tonnes (267,859lb)	124 tonnes (273,370lb)
Max fuel capacity	75,470 lit (19,940 US gal)	75,470 lit (19,940 US gal)
Engines	2x JT9D-7R4 / GE CF6-80 Turbofan (2 x 57,900lbf)	2x JT9D-7R4E1 / PW4000 / CF6-80C2 Turbofan (2 x 62,000lbf)
Typical cruise speed	M.069	M.072
Max flight level	41,100ft	41,000ft

Source: Airbus

ABOVE • *Spain's Plus Ultra Líneas Aéreas operates a fleet of two A340-300s and two A340-600s on routes to South America and the Caribbean.* ALEC WILSON, FLICKR

LEFT • *An A300-600F takes off destined for Fed Express.* AIRBUS-IMAGE EXM COMPANY-P.MASCLET

A340 family technical specifications

	A340-200	A340-300	A340-500	A340-600
Length	59.4m (194ft 11in)	63.69m (208ft 11in)	67.93m (222ft 10in)	75.36m (247ft 3in)
Height	16.8m (55ft 1in)	16.99m (55ft 9in)	17.53m (57ft 6in)	17.93m (58ft 10in)
Fuselage width	5.64m (18ft 6in)	5.28m (17ft 4in)	5.64m (18ft 6in)	5.64m (18ft 6in)
Wingspan	60.3m (197ft 10in)	60.3m (197ft 10in)	63.45m (208ft 2in)	63.45m (208ft 2in)
Passengers (max)	420	440	440	475
Cabin length	46.06m (151ft 1in)	50.35m (165ft 2in)	53.56m (175ft 9in)	60.98m (200ft 1in)
Max cabin width	5.28m (17ft 4in)	5.28m (17ft 4in)	5.28m (17ft 4in)	5.28m (17ft 4in)
Cabin Height	2.54m (8ft 4in)	2.54m (8ft 4in)	2.54m (8ft 4in)	2.54m (8ft 4in)
Max take-off weight	275 tonnes (606,300lb)	276.5 tonnes (609,600lb)	380 tonnes (837,800lb)	380 tonnes (837,800lb)
Max landing weight	181 tonnes (399,000lb)	192 tonnes (423,300lb)	246 tonnes (542,300lb)	265 tonnes (584,200lb)
Max fuel capacity	155,040 lit (36,678 US gal)	147,850 lit (39,060 US gal)	222,850 lit (58,875 US gal)	204,500 lit (54,020 US gal)
Engines	4 x CFM International CFM56-5C Turbofan (4 x 34,000lbf)	4 x CFM International CFM56-5C Turbofan (4 x 34,000lbf)	4 x Rolls Royce Trent 553 Turbofan (4 x 54,000lbf)	4 X Rolls Royce Trent 556 Turbofan (4 x 61.902lbf)
Typical cruise speed	M.086	M.086	M.086	M.086
Max flight level	41,000ft	41,000ft	41,450ft	41,450ft

Source: Airbus

ABOVE • *Virgin Atlantic's first ever Airbus aircraft was the A340.* MIKE MCBEY

RIGHT • *Sri Lankan, the first Asian airline to operate the A340 retired the aircraft in 2016, after 21 years of service.* ALLEN WATKIN

RIGHT • *Iranian Mahan Air used the A340 to develop new international routes to Europe and Asia.* ALEX WILSON

BELOW • *Edelweiss uses A340s inherited from SWISS for long-haul flights from its Zurich base.* EDELWEISS

route, the higher operating costs of the A340 left it adrift.

Its fate was sealed in 2008 when the price of jet fuel doubled and long-haul economics forced some airlines to look for shorter routes, particularly for the A340. As an example, in 2008 Thai International cancelled its nonstop Bangkok to New York flight and decided to sell its A340s.

On November 10, 2011, Airbus announced it was ending the A340 program and said that it had delivered all the firm orders for the aircraft. The A340 was launched in 1987 and closed in 2011, with 377 aircraft delivered to airlines in that time.

As of April 2025, there are around 80 A340s still active, with Lufthansa holding 17 A340-300s and ten A340-600s. The -600s were sent to storage when the COVID-19 pandemic hit but returned to service, due to delays with new aircraft deliveries. Lufthansa plans to retire its A340 fleet by 2028.

Legacy

The A330, A310 and A340 are an indelible part of the Airbus story and without them new-generation aircraft like the A330neo, A350 XWB and A380

may not have made it off the Toulouse drawing boards.

They were the means to breaking into the extremely tough US market and the right fit for today's large Asian

and Middle East carriers when they were starting to develop commercial aviation. These three aircraft live on, and travellers all around the globe are reaping the benefits of that today.

ABOVE • *Air Astana operates some of the youngest 767s on it long haul routes from Almaty and Astana to Bangkok, Frankfurt, Kuala Lumpur, and Seoul.* AIR ASTANA

LEFT • *Delta has long supported Breast Cancer Awareness. The Boeing 767-400ER has featured a pink-themed livery since 2010. The "Pink Plane" flies with a cabin full of employees who have survived breast cancer or are battling the disease.* DELTA

The Twinjet Age

The 767 and 777 heralded a new age in transatlantic travel, with Boeing adopting new approaches to their design and manufacture.

Not content with dealing with the complexities of designing and producing one aircraft type at any one time, in the early 1970s Boeing decided to embark on a parallel programme of designing the widebody 767, and narrowbody 757.

The company hoped that the new 767 would appeal to those operators upgrading from the 727 or Lockheed TriStar's and McDonnell Douglas DC-10s. Internally, it was seen as direct competition to the A300 and A310 from Airbus, which had begun to make inroads into the US market. And with fuel prices rocketing at that time, the main selling point of the new aircraft was fuel efficiency - with Boeing looking for up to 30% cost savings over previous aircraft, through the use of computer-aided design, new engines, and wing technology.

In a departure from precedent for new aircraft, early customers were offered a choice of engine options – either the Pratt & Whitney JT9D or General Electric CF6 turbofans,

However, it took much of the 1970s for the 767 to move off the drawing board and into development, the first protype flying in 1981, three years after the programme officially began. Certification was achieved the following year in 1982 and just two months later United Airlines became the launch customer.

Over a 23-year period, from 1982 until 2005, United would own 19 767-200s, before inheriting a further 10 former Continental 767-200ERS in 2012, as a result of their merger. Unlike their original fleet, which predominantly served the routes from New York JFK to Los Angeles and San Francisco, the -200ERs continued to be used for intercontinental flights out of Huston and Newark.

The 767

Boeing's first twinjet, the 767 was built in Everett, Washington, which had been extended to accommodate the new widebody family alongside the 747. Its two-crew glass cockpit, a first for a Boeing airliner, was developed jointly for the 757 – a narrow-body aircraft, allowing a common pilot type rating. The cockpit also includes digital avionics EFIS (manufactured by Rockwell-Collins) with six multifunctional colour screens.

With ETOPS (Extended-range Twin-engine Operational Performance Standards) approval in 1985, regular flights across the Atlantic now became commonplace. At the peak of production in 1992, a new Boeing 767 was rolled out on average every six days, as the 767 became the go-to aircraft for transatlantic flights. By the time production of the original 767-200 ceased, some 128 aircraft had been delivered.

In 1984, Boeing introduced the -200ER, with El Al the launch customer. The ability to fly longer routes is due to the use of the centre tank's dry dock to carry fuel, and a higher maximum take-off weight (MTOW). Showcasing its extended range, in 1988 a 767-200ER operated by Air Mauritius became a record beaker for a twinjet when it flew nonstop from Halifax, Nova Scotia, Canada to the Mauritian capital Port Louis, a distance of 16,200km.

Other variants include the stretched version -300, introduced by Japan Airlines in 1986 and the -300ER introduced with American Airlines in 1988. Design improvements made it possible to increase the MTOW and fuel capacity, allowing for the greater range.

In December 2019, Delta began operating flights between New York and Los Angeles with Boeing 767-300 aircraft – rather than a mix of different aircraft types – making Delta the only airline to offer a consistent, all-widebody cabin experience on the competitive route. The change meant that all customers seated in the Delta One cabin have direct aisle access. Delta Comfort+ and Main Cabin feature a 2-3-2 seat configuration, meaning fewer middle seats and more space.

At the same time, Delta introduced its refurbished 767-400 fleet, with flights departing New York-JFK and Boston for London-Heathrow, JFK, and Brussels, Nice, and Zurich, and JFK to Sao Paulo.

Throughout 2019, United also reconfigured its 767-300ER fleet. The reconfigured Boeing 767-300ER aircraft features 16 additional United Polaris business-class seats – a more than 50% increase in all-aisle-access seating – bringing the total premium cabin seat count to 46. The aircraft will also feature 22 United Premium Plus seats, 47 Economy Plus seats and 52 Economy seats. United operates the reconfigured 767 between Newark/New York and London.

In 2000, Continental Airlines became the launch customer of the 767-400ER, which had its fuselage and wingspan increased as well as redesigned landing gear and updated cockpit.

The popularity of the 767 is waning though. In February 2011, the Everett factory produced its 1,000th 767. Over a decade later and slow sales has led to just 238 more being produced as of May 2022.

In December 1991, Boeing offered a modified 767 commercial jetliner as the platform for its Airborne Warning and Control System (AWACS), previously carried aboard the 707. The first of the 767 AWACS, designated E-767, made its first flight August 9, 1996, and the government of Japan ordered four of them. Then, in 2000, Boeing launched its international 767 tanker/transport. The Italian Air Force and the Japan Air Self-Defense Force became customers

In February 2011. the US Air Force awarded a contract to Boeing to develop a tanker to replace its aging KC-135 fleet. Based on the 767-2C, a freighter version of the 767-200ER, the new KC-46 Pegasus is able to refuel 64 different aircraft and can detect, avoid, defeat, and survive threats using multiple layers of protection. The US Air Force took delivery of its first two KC-46A tankers in December 2018.

The 767 is the only Boeing product that serves the freighter, passenger, and tanker markets.

Boeing 767 technical specifications

	767-200	767-220ER	767-300	767-300ER	767-400ER
Length	48.5m (159ft 1in)	54.94m (180ft 3in)	54.94m (180ft 3in)	54.94m (180ft 3in)	61.4m (201ft 44in)
Height	16.13m (52ft 11in)	16.03m (52ft 7in)	16.03m (52ft 7in)	16.03m (52ft 7in)	16.80m (55ft .12in)
Fuselage width	5.03m (16ft 6in)	5.03m (16ft 6in)	5.03m (16ft 6in)	5.03m (16ft 6in)	5.03m (16ft 6in)
Wingspan	47.6m (156ft 2in)	47.57m (156ft 1in)	47.57m (156ft 1in)	47.57m (156ft 1in)	51.9m (170ft .27in)
Passengers (max)	290	351	351	351	351
Cabin length	33.93m (111ft 4in)	40.36m (132ft 5in)	40.36m (132ft 5in)	40.36m (132ft 5in)	40.36m (132ft 5in)
Max cabin width	4.7m (15ft 5in)	4.72m (15ft 6in)	4.72m (15ft 6in)	4.72m (15ft 6in)	4.72m (15ft 6in)
Cabin Height	2.10m (6ft 11in)	2.87m (9ft 5in)	2.87m (9ft 5in)	2.87m (9ft 5in)	2.87m (9ft 5in)
Max take-off weight	142 tonnes (314,998lb)	179.2 tonnes (395,000lb)	158 tonnes (349,998lb)	184 tonnes (407,000lb)	158 tonnes (349,998lb)
Max landing weight	123 tonnes (271,997lb)	136 tonnes (299,998lb)	136 tonnes (299,998lb)	136 tonnes (299,998lb)	136 tonnes (299,998lb)
Max fuel capacity	63,216 lit (16,700 US gal)	63,216 lit (16,700 US gal)	63,216 lit (16,700 US gal)	63,216 lit (16,700 US gal)	63,216 lit (16,700 US gal)
Engines	2x General Electric CF6-80C2, Pratt & Whitney JT9D Turbofan (2 x 60,600lbf)	2x Rolls Royce RB211-524H or General Electric CF6-80C2B or Pratt & Whitney PW4060 Turbofan (2 x 60,600lbf)	2x Rolls Royce RB211-524H or General Electric CF6-80C2B or Pratt & Whitney PW4060 Turbofan (2 x 60,600lbf)	2x Rolls Royce RB211-524H or General Electric CF6-80C2B or Pratt & Whitney PW4060 Turbofan (2 x 60,600lbf)	2x Pratt and Whitney PW4000-94 or General Electric CF6-80C2B7F1 Turbofan (2 x 63,300lbf)
Typical cruise speed	M.074	M.070	M.073		M.074
Max flight level	43,200ft	43,000ft	43,000ft	43,000ft	43,000ft

Source: Boeing

Boeing 777 technical specifications

	777-200ER	777-200LR	777-300	777-300ER
Length	63.7m (209ft)	63.7m (209ft)	73.9m (242ft 5in)	73.9m (242ft 5in)
Height	18.5m (60ft 8in)	18.6m (61ft)	18.5m (60ft 8in)	18.5m (60ft 8in)
Fuselage width	6.19m (20ft 4in)	6.19m (20ft 4in)	6.19m (20ft 4in)	6.19m (20ft 4in)
Wingspan	60.9m (199ft 10in)	64.8m (212ft 7in)	60.9m (199ft 10in)	64.8m (212ft 7in)
Passengers (max)	440	440	550	550
Cabin length	49.1m (161ft 1in)	49.1m (161ft 1in)	59.24m (194ft 4in)	59.24m (194ft 4in)
Max cabin width	5.86m (19ft 3in)	5.86m (19ft 3in)	5.86m (19ft 3in)	5.86m (19ft 3in)
Cabin Height	2.2m (7ft 3in)	2.2m (7ft 3in)	2.2m (7ft 3in)	2.2m (7ft 3in)
Max take-off weight	297 tonnes (655,979lb)	347 tonnes (765,993lb)	299 tonnes (659,991lb)	351 tonnes (774,994lb)
Max landing weight	213 tonnes (469,977lb)	223 tonnes (491,996lb)	N/A	260 tonnes (574,995lb)
Max fuel capacity	171,176 lit (45,220 US gal)	181,283 lit (47,890 US gal)	171,176 lit (45,220 US gal)	181,283 lit (47,890 US gal)
Engines	2x Pratt and Whitney PW 4090 or Rolls-Royce Trent 895 or GE GE90-94B Turbofan (2 x 93,700lbf)	2x General Electric GE90-115B Turbofan (2 x 115.300lbf)	2x Rolls Royce RR-892 or Pratt & Whitney 4098 or GE90-94B Turbofan (2 x 98,000lbf)	2x Rolls Royce RR-892 or Pratt & Whitney 4098 or GE90-94B Turbofan (2 x 98,000lbf)
Typical cruise speed	M.077	M.077	M.077	M.077
Max flight level	43,000ft	43,100ft	43,100ft	43,100ft

Source: Boeing

ABOVE • *The Everett, Washington State facility, site of the manufacture of the 777. Boeing later introduced an ill-fated automated robotic system to manufacture the fuselage at the site.* GAIL HANUSA

ABOVE RIGHT • *An Emirates 777-300ER. The airline also operates the 777-200LR.* EMIRATES

RIGHT • *A SWISS 777.* SWISS

777

To many observers, it seemed like a folly for Boeing to consider developing a new widebody model, given the success and popularity of the 747. But with the introduction of the 777, Boeing struck gold once again.

Often referred to as the 'Triple Seven', it was the world's first commercial aircraft entirely designed by computer. Throughout the design process, the airplane was 'preassembled' on the computer, eliminating the need for a costly, full-scale mock-up.

The 777 was larger than all other twinjet or trijet airplanes but smaller than the 747 and included improvements in airfoil technology, flight deck design, passenger comfort, and interior flexibility. Its visible features include super large engines, low hanging landing gear and a blade shaped tail cone with a relatively narrow tailfin.

ABOVE • *Lufthansa 777.*
OLIVER ROESLER

In 2014, Boeing introduced a new method for building 777 fuselages. The Fuselage Automated Upright Build, or FAUB, saw sections built using automated, guided robots to fasten the panels of the fuselage together, drilling and filling the more than approximately 60,000 fasteners that are today installed by hand.

The robotic system, designed for Boeing by KUKA Systems, was intended to improve employee safety as more than half of all injuries on the 777 programme occurred during the phase of production that was being automated. In addition, the automated system was expected to reduce build times and improve first-time quality of the build process. However, five years after its introduction, Boeing abandoned the process, after dealing with numerous instances of damaged fuselages and incomplete assembly.

United Airlines became the launch customer for the 777 in 1990, using the Pratt and Whitney PW400 engine. Then, on November 12, 1995, Boeing delivered the first model with General Electric GE90-77B engines to British Airways, and in March 1996, Thai Airways International took delivery of the first Rolls-Royce Trent 877-powered aircraft.

In April 2019, Emirates completed the year-long reconfiguration of its Boeing 777-200LR aircraft, part of a $150m conversion programme, which saw 10 Boeing 777-200LR aircraft in its fleet converted from three to two class cabins featuring wider business-class seats in a 2-2-2 format and a fully refreshed economy-class cabin. The programme was conducted in-house at Emirates Engineering's state of the art facilities in Dubai. The engineering team spent a total of over 160,000 man-hours on the project, working with more than 30 suppliers and handling over 2,700 spare parts at any one time. On average it took 35 days for the team to completely strip and reconfigure a single aircraft.

Emirates has also retired the last two Boeing 777-300 classic aircraft in its fleet. A6-EMV, delivered in February 2003, has

Alongside seven other airline counterparts, British Airways took part in the design of the aircraft. In 2006, British Airways set a new record for the longest non-stop commercial flight. The Boeing 777-200 flew 17,157km (9,274nm) from Brussels to Melbourne, in 18 hours and 45 minutes.

The untraditional and collaborative design approach included input from All Nippon Airways, American, Cathay Pacific, Delta, Japan Airlines, Qantas and United, with each bringing their own requirements to the table and ultimately the final design.

Key features include flexible interiors, a glass cockpit, and fly-by-wire controls. In total, the aircraft has three million parts provided by more than 900 global suppliers.

BELOW • *Boeing reaches a milestone with the rollout of the 1,000th 767.* BOEING

BELOW • *A new JAL 767 takes to the air at Paine Field in Everett, Washington for its ferry flight to Narita Airport in Japan.* BOEING

ABOVE • *An El Al 777.*
BOEING

LEFT • *Qatar Airways 777.*
QATAR AIRWAYS

now been phased out of the Emirates fleet as has A6-EMX, delivered in June 2003. With the retirement of the 777-300 classic aircraft, Emirates' Boeing fleet will be composed of the Boeing 777-300ER and the newly refreshed Boeing 777-200LRs.

By 2014, the 777 was available in six models: the 777-200; 777-200ER (Extended Range); a larger 777-300, launched at the Paris Air Show on June 26, 1995, and subsequently debuted by Cathay Pacific; two longer range models, the 777-300ER, which rolled out on November 14, 2002, entering into commercial service with Air France in 2002; the 777-200LR Worldliner (the world's longest range commercial airplane) and the Boeing 777 Freighter.

The 777 family has proved itself to be popular and much loved. It is the bestselling widebody jet of all time. The impending introduction of the 777X, (777-9) will give passengers the flight experience of the future. Though only once production delays have been addressed.

ABOVE • *Biman Bangladesh's first 777, a 777-300ER.* BOEING

RIGHT • *The 777 is a favourite among Middle Eastern operators.* BOEING

BELOW • *A Turkish Airlines 777.* BOEING

The BIG Jets

The four-engine 747 and A380 are the Hercules of the skies.
Michael Doran looks at how these two aircraft match up.

Aircraft like the Boeing 747 and the Airbus A380 are almost impossible to meaningfully compare. The 747 was conceived in the 1960s to capitalise on the surging demand for air travel, while the A380 was a 1990s answer to slot-constrained airports and airline hub and spoke networks.

The 747 was virtually a clean sheet design, built around the needs of Boeing's major customer, Pan American Airways, and their push to radically reduce seat-mile costs on longer flights. It was going from a 707 with around 180 seats to a two-storey jumbo with 400 passengers.

Thankfully, the 747 designers and engineers were up to the task and produced a beautiful and graceful aircraft that ruled the skies for nearly 30 years. Flying on a 747 was special and generally left people wondering how on earth such a big aircraft could so effortlessly take to the air.

Thirty years after the 747 first carried paying passengers, Airbus launched its A380 programme, in a time when technology, economics, politics and passenger expectations were vastly different to those that Boeing had faced in the 1970s.

The neat thing is that Airbus did not set out to match the 747, they looked at what they saw was needed and designed their own solution, a double-decker bus that could easily carry 600 people across continents and oceans.

The A380 is a magnificent piece of modern engineering that brought disparate aircraft manufacturers together under the Airbus banner, with sections being made in the UK, Spain, Germany, and France. Insiders at Airbus say this was the making of the Airbus we see today, an international leader in commercial aviation, defence, and aerospace industries.

The A380 also introduced Airbus to the concept of developing aircraft as a family of different sizes for different customer needs. It's why Airbus designed the Airspace Cabin, which gives passengers a consistent experience, look and feel whether they are flying an A320, A330, A350 or A380.

What can't be lost in any discussion of the 747 and A380 is the enormous contribution of the engine makers, General Electric, Pratt & Whitney, and Rolls-Royce. Every time Airbus or Boeing started to develop a new aircraft the engine OEMs have risen to the challenge of designing more powerful engines that also reduce CO_2 emissions. The reality is that the 10% to 15% fuel burn and emission reductions that the aircraft manufacturers promote are mostly coming from the advances in engine technology.

Both the 747 and the A380 have their own unique story to tell, and they were never really competing with each other. When one was in its twilight the other was being born and together they have spanned more than half a century of pioneering aviation development. Here is how they did it. 

LEFT • *The 747 was the result of the work of 50,000 Boeing employees, lovingly known as 'the Incredibles'.* COLLIN COOKE

BELOW • *British Airways celebrated its centenary with a series of heritage livery designs. This British Overseas Airways Corporation (BOAC) 747 will fly until its retirement in 2023.* STUART BAILEY/ BRITISH AIRWAYS

The Boeing 747

The jumbo jet era arrived on January 22, 1970 when the first commercial flight of the Boeing 747 left New York for London, operated by launch customer Pan Am. While the 747 is credited with opening up air travel to the masses, it was more a case on building on what the 707 and DC-8 had achieved in the 1960s.

The jumbo certainly ushered in affordable air travel, which previously had been the province of the more wealthy and powerful sections of the community. A cramped metal tube gave way to a wide, spacious cabin with an upper deck that was a mystery to most of the 400 passengers on board.

Passengers on the end of global routes, such as in Africa, South America, Asia, and Australia now had an affordable way to connect with Europe and North America. Journeys that typically involved a handful of transits were now cut in half, switching people from ships to the air.

In the early 1970s a Qantas trip from Melbourne to London involved transit stops in Sydney, Singapore, Bangkok, Bahrain, and Frankfurt. Within a few years that was down to a single stop in Singapore before arriving at London's Heathrow Airport.

Long-haul airlines like Qantas, Air New Zealand, British Airways, Pan Am, Singapore Airlines and Cathay Pacific built their networks around what the 747 could deliver, especially in opening up new tourist markets that were not viable with a 707 or DC-8. So, how did the Queen of the Skies come about?

ABOVE LEFT • *The 747's final departure with United was dubbed the 'Friend Ship', the same name given to the original flight over the Pacific.* UNITED AIRLINES

BELOW • *The 747-8F variant of US freight carrier Atlas Air, the operator of the world's largest fleet of 747 freighter aircraft.* ATLAS AIR

ABOVE • *'Ed Force One':
Iron Maiden's flying
tour bus. Not quite as
presidential as 'Air Force
One', but certainly more
rock n'roll.* ERIC BAUER

The Boeing 747 was a child of the 1960s, a time when the 707 and Douglas DC-8 had changed the face of commercial aviation. Air travel was becoming more accessible as incomes rose and ticket prices came down, a reflection of the larger and more fuel-efficient aircraft that airlines such as Pan Am began to operate.

The 707 first flew in 1957 and between 1956 and 1978, 865 of them were built for customers including Trans World Airlines, Pan Am, American Airlines, and Air France. The 707 dominated commercial air travel through the 1960s, on domestic, transcontinental, and transatlantic flights.

The success of the 707 and the Douglas DC-8 led to rapid developments in the aviation environment, including in airports, catering, baggage handling and reservation systems. As the public embraced jet travel, the 707 became too small

BELOW • *The tail fin of
an A380.* GOUSSE HERVE -
MASTERFILMS

and Boeing, encouraged by Pan Am, turned its attention to the developing the 747.

In the early 1960s Pan Am had asked Boeing to design a bigger aircraft and design of the 747 picked up speed around 1965. In April 1966, Pan Am ordered 25 Boeing 747-100 aircraft, with Boeing agreeing that the first would be delivered by the end of 1969.

The first flight took place in February 1969, with the 747 achieving FAA certification in December of that year. On January 15, 1970, Pan Am's 747-100 was christened by the First Lady of the United States, Pat Nixon at Dulles International Airport and it entered service on January 22, 1970, on Pan Am's signature New York-London service.

The 747-100 typically carried 366 passengers in a three-class layout with a range of 4,620nm (8,560km) and had a cockpit crew of two pilots and a flight engineer. Other variants included the 747-200B, 747-300, 747SP and the 747-400, the latter becoming the most popular version of the aircraft that was now known as the jumbo.

Development of the longer range 747-400 began in 1985 and the new variant entered service in 1989. The -400 had a new glass cockpit which reduced the flight crew to the two pilots, a range of 7,285-7,670nm (13,492-14,205km) and a three-class capacity of around 416 passengers.

The final iteration is the 747-8, which was considered to be Boeing's alternative to the Airbus A380. The 747-8 fuselage was stretched by 18ft (5.5m) to 250ft (76m), making it the longest commercial airliner until the Boeing 777X took the title away in 2020. The 747-8 also had a new engine, the General Electric GEnx-2B67 and the aircraft comes in two variants, the -8I passenger and the -8F freighter aircraft.

The freighter was the first to fly in February 2010 and entered service with Cargolux on October 12, 2011. The -8I, (Intercontinental), had its first flight in March 2011 and

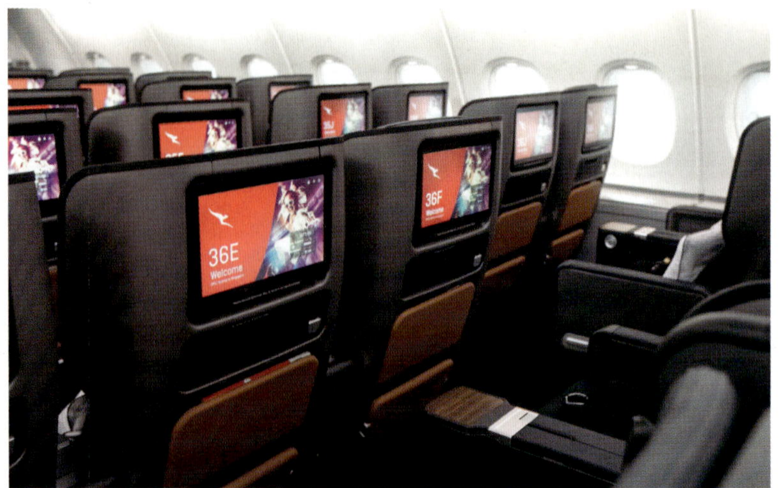

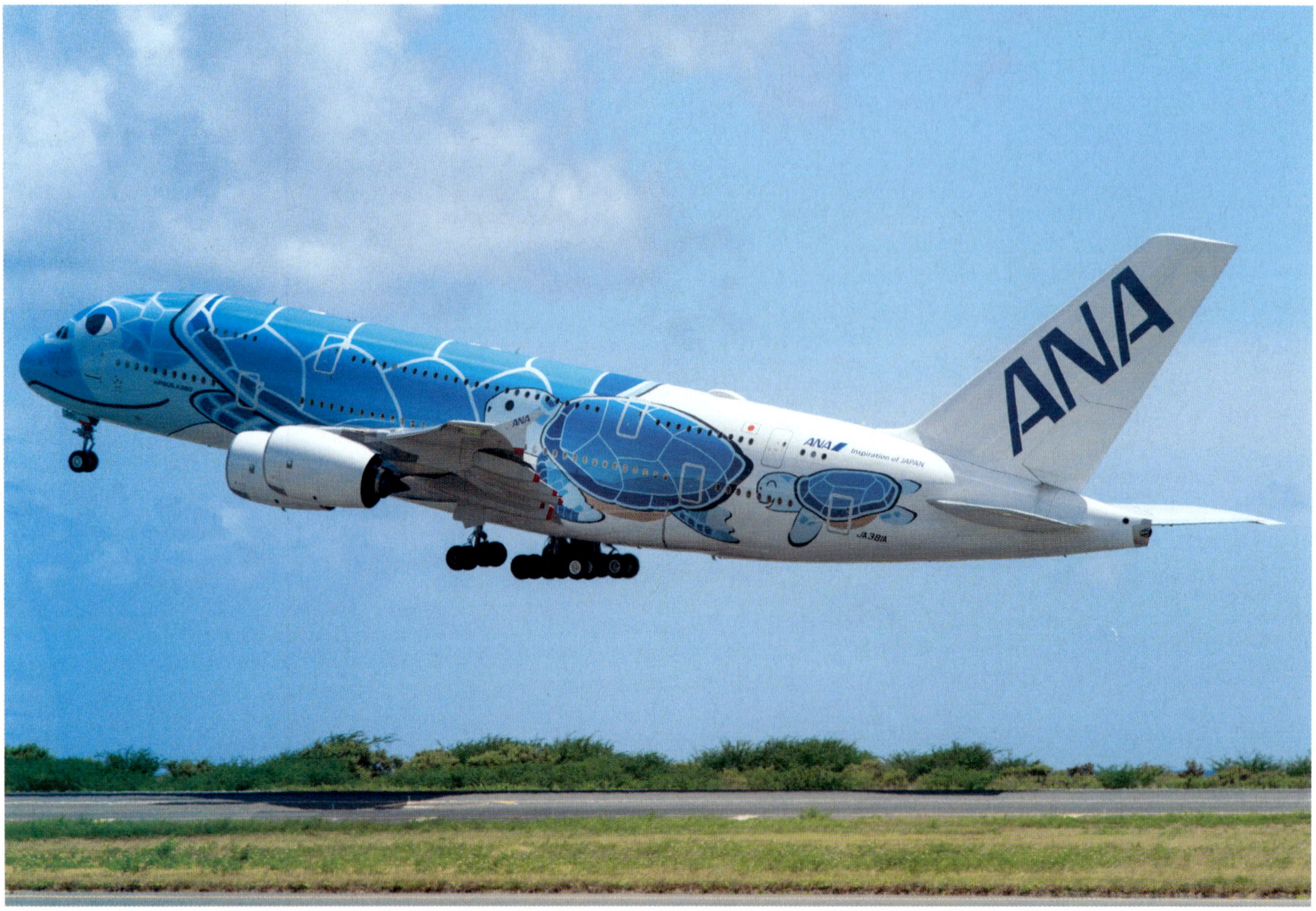

entered service with Lufthansa on June 1, 2012. The 747-8I has a range of 7,730nm (14,320km) in a three-class layout of 467 passengers, while the 747-8Fs range is 4,265nm (7,899km).

By April 2022, Boeing had gained 155 orders for 747-8s, of which 151 have been delivered. There are four unfilled orders for 747-8F aircraft which are to be delivered to Atlas Air Worldwide Holdings. Around 70% of orders have been for the freighter version, which is in use with major logistics operators including UPS Airlines, Cargolux, Cathay Pacific Cargo, and Korean Air.

The two highest profile 747-8Is are the pair currently being converted to operate as *Air Force One*, the aircraft used to transport the President of the United States. The pair were originally ordered by a Russian airline, Transaero and are currently being converted by Boeing.

In a 2018 handshake deal with then-president Donald Trump, Boeing agreed to a fixed price contract of $3.9bn (£3.2bn) and by 2020 it reported it had already lost around $1.5bn on the deal. The aircraft are due to be delivered two years late, in 2025 and 2027.

Before COVID-19 arrived and finished off the 747, many airlines, including Cathay Pacific, United Airlines and Delta Air Lines had already retired their 747 fleets. Some were given momentous final-flight send offs but most just made that lonely journey to an aircraft boneyard in an American desert.

US carrier United Airlines did it in style, recreating its first 747 flight which had taken place on July 23, 1970 from San Francisco to Honolulu. On November 7, 2017 United's final 747 flight was from San Francisco to Honolulu, where passengers were greeted with lei garlands, Hawaiian music and hula dancers.

These large aircraft inspire airlines to develop new aircraft, not necessarily to match the competition but usually to surpass what they are doing. The 747 owned the long-haul market for close to 30 years and set the bar for what an airliner should feel like, more private jet than metal tube.

The Airbus A380

In 2019 when Airbus announced it was ceasing production of the A380, opinions were divided on how the programme should be assessed and what would be the legacy of the revolutionary aircraft.

Its supporters, and many of its passengers, pointed to the A380's size, comfort, and efficiency in moving around 600 people as markers of its success. Its critics pointed to sales of just 251 aircraft as proof it was a flop and a giant economic failure.

With development costs estimated to be around £20-£25bn ($25-$30bn), well beyond the initial Airbus estimate of £9bn, and its relatively short programme life do give critics scope for their derision.

ABOVE • ***The first FLYING HONU entered service on the Narita-Honolulu route in May 2019, painted in blue to represent the Hawaiian blue sky.*** AERO ICARUS/FLICKR

BELOW • ***Qantas revamped its A380 interior before the COVID-19 pandemic. It has begun the reactivation process into service following their enforced storage.*** QANTAS

Boeing 747 and A380 design specifications

	747-100	747-400	747-800	A380-800
Length	70.6m (231ft 8in)	70.6m (231ft 8in)	76.3.m (250ft.20in)	72.7m (238ft 6in)
Height	19.3m (63ft 4in)	19.3m (63ft 4in)	19.4m (63ft 8in)	24.1m (79ft 1 in)
Fuselage width	6.5m (21ft 4in)	6.49m (21ft 4in)	6.49m (21ft 4in)	7.1m (23ft 4in)
Wingspan	59.6m (195ft 6in)	59.6m (195ft 6in)	64.4m (211ft 3in)	79.75m (261ft 8in)
Passengers (max)	366	416	467	853
Cabin length	50.5m (165ft 8in)	57m (187ft)	63.25m (207ft 6in)	50.68m (166ft 3in)
Max cabin width	6.1m (20ft)	6.1m (20ft)	6.1m (20ft)	6.58m (21ft 7in)
Cabin Height	3.1m (10ft 2in)	2.54m (8ft 4in)	2.39m (7ft 10in)	3m (9ft 11in)
Max take-off weight	333 tonnes (735,000lb)	396 tonnes (874,894lb)	447 tonnes (986,991lb)	575 tonnes (1,267.645lb)
Max landing weight	265 tonnes (585,000lb)	295 tonnes (651,988lb)	312 tonnes (687,994lb)	394 tonnes (870,817lb)
Max zero fuel weight	172 tonnes (379,500lb)	183 tonnes (404,600lb)	220 tonnes (485,300lb)	361 tonnes (795,869lb)
Max fuel capacity	183,380 lit (48,445 US gal)	199,158 lit (52,410 US gal)	238,069 lit (63,034 US gal)	320,000 lit (85,472 US gal)
Engines	4x Pratt & Whitney JT9D-7 or Rolls-Royce RB211-524 or GE CF6 Turbofan (4 x 51.600lbf)	4x P&W4000 / GE CF6 / RR RB211 Turbofan (4 x 63.300lbf)	4x General Electric GEnx 2B67 Turbofan (4 s 66,500lbf)	4x Engine Alliance GP7270 or Rolls-Royce Trent 900 Turbofan (4 x 81,500lbf)
Typical cruise speed	M.078	M.078	M.082	M.085
Max flight level	45,100ft	45,000ft	43,000ft	43,000ft

Source: Airbus, Boeing

BELOW • *A Cathay Pacific Airways 747-8 Freighter was the first 747 delivered with performance-improved GEnx-2B engines as part of the airplane's Performance Improvement Package (PIP).* BOEING

BRITISH

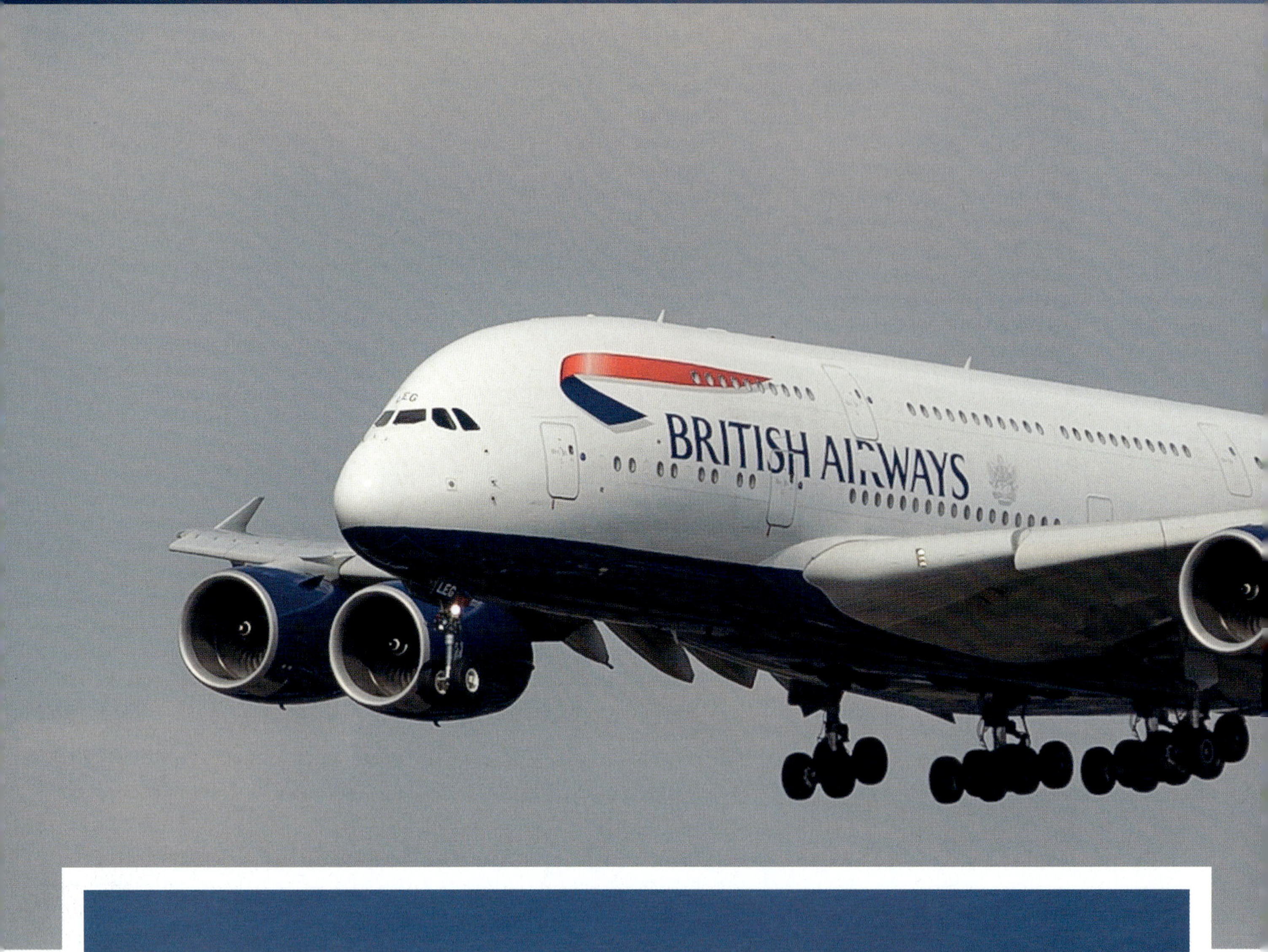

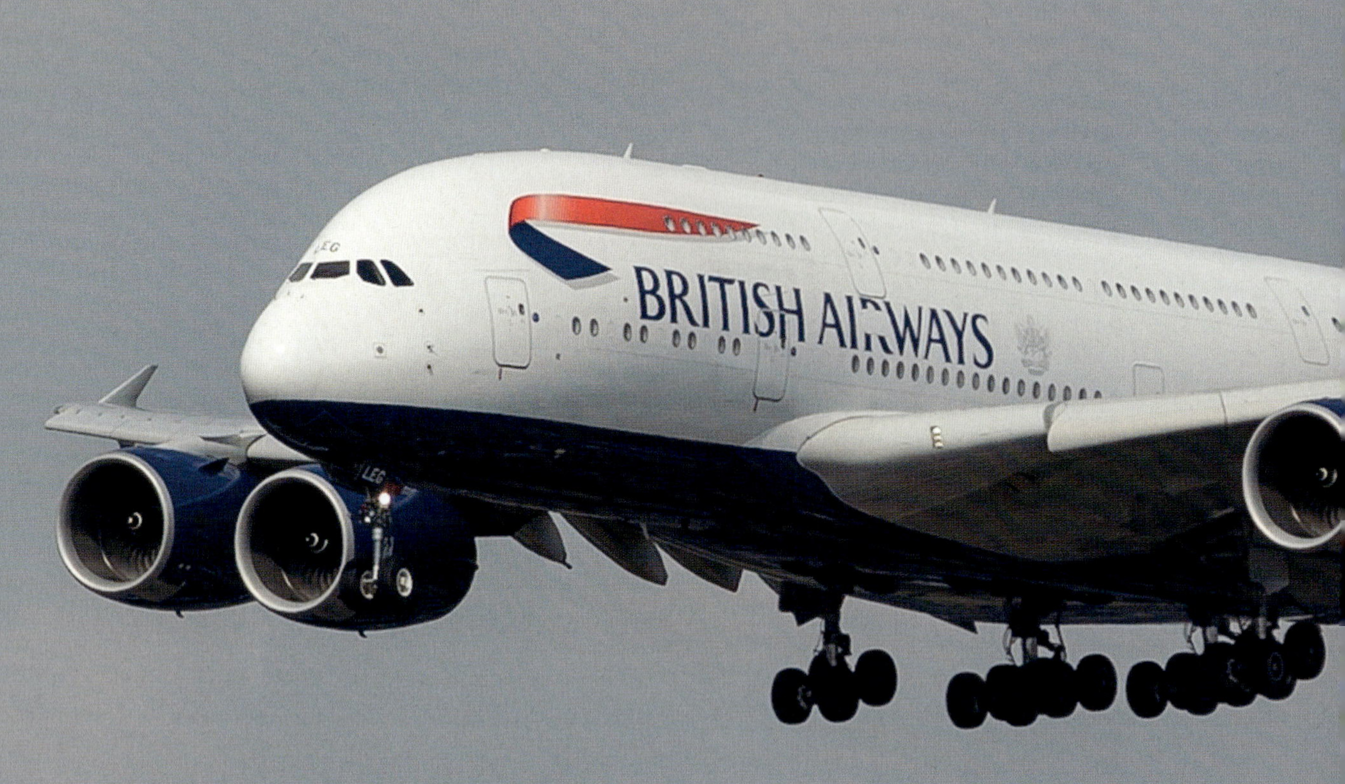

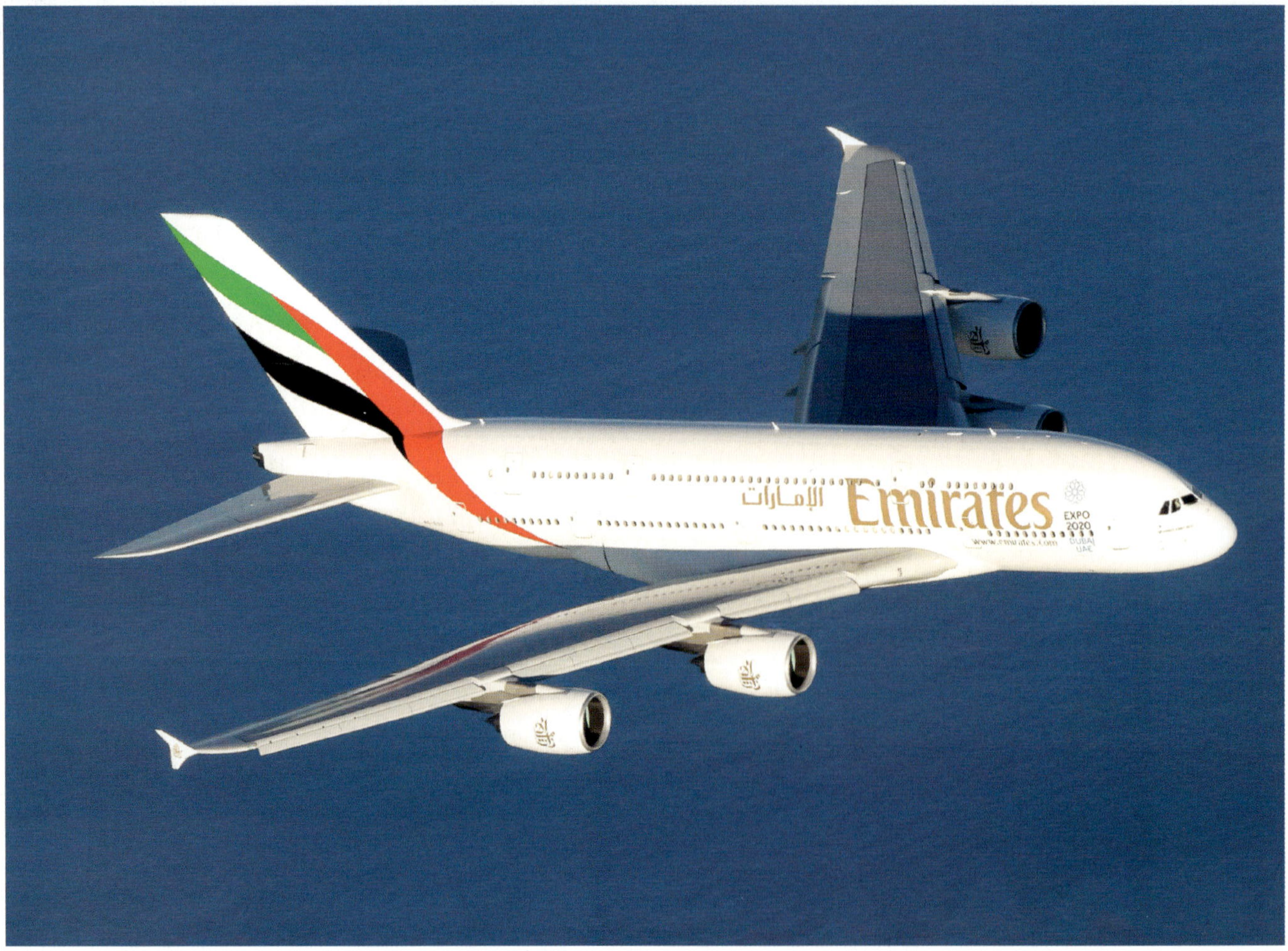
الإمارات
Emirates
EXPO
2020

ABOVE • *A British Airways A380 coming into land.* NICK MORRISH/BRITISH AIRWAYS

LEFT • *Over 131m passengers have flown on an Emirates A380 since 2007.* EMIRATES

However, the programme's value goes well beyond the A380 itself, with today's leading aircraft, like the A350 and A321 LR, benefiting from technologies developed for the 'super jumbo', so its legacy lives on.

It's also important to look at the A380 in the context of when it was designed, and the markets Airbus was planning to conquer with the new airplane. Within Airbus the search for a 747 challenger started in the late 1980s, with the A3XX project surfacing in 1994.

Airbus launched the A380 program in December 2000 and in just five years, five A380s had been built, with the first flight happening on April 27, 2005. The aircraft was certified by both the FAA and EASA on December 12, 2006 and the first delivery was to Singapore Airlines in October 2007. The first commercial flight, SQ380, was from Singapore to Sydney, Australia on October 25, 2006.

Various airframe and engine production delays resulted in Airbus renegotiating delivery schedules and compensating 13 customers, including Emirates, Singapore Airlines, Qantas, Air France, Qatar Airways and Korean Air.

The second A380 went to Emirates, who launched it on the Dubai-New York route in August 2008, followed by Qantas on the Melbourne-Los Angeles service in October of the same year. By the end of 2008, the A380 had operated 2,200 flights and carried around 890,000 passengers.

Emirates is the largest A380 operator with 93 in its fleet and its support has been pivotal to the success of aircraft, having taken close to half of all the A380s produced. Emirates, Etihad Airways and Qatar Airways have used the A380 in a classic hub and spoke model, where the airlines transfer passengers at their Middle East hubs from one long-haul flight to another.

With small populations this was the only way for these carriers to grow market share and the A380 perfectly suited their operational and aspirational needs. Qantas switched its transfer hubs from Singapore and Hong Kong to Dubai for their London A380 flights. Although that changed when Qantas launched direct flights from Perth to London using the Boeing 787 Dreamliner and abandoned its Dubai transit hub altogether.

British Airways, Korean Air, Lufthansa, China Southern Airlines and Singapore Airlines are other legacy carriers who favoured the A380 on long-haul routes. In the case of China Southern, the super jumbo was the right size for its busiest domestic flights, such as Shanghai-Beijing, as well as on international routes to Europe, Australia, and the US.

In 2019 All Nippon Airways began flying direct from Tokyo to Honolulu with the first of three A380s it had ordered. Again, this was a point-to-point route where the seating capacity of the A380 suited the high volumes of Japanese and American tourists who travel between the two destinations.

Interestingly, when borders reopened post-COVID-19 in 2022, it was the A380 that long haul airlines such as Qantas, Singapore Airlines, Emirates and Qatar recalled as they scrambled to meet passenger demand.

Qantas has a dozen A380s and when the pandemic hit in 2020 it sent them off for parking in a US desert boneyard, rather unfortunately this was just after the

carrier had spent millions on refurbishing the interiors on some of the aircraft. In the space of a few months three of them were back in service operating direct services from Australia to Europe, Asia, and the US. By the end of 2025, ten will have returned to the skies, with two having been dismantled for spare parts.

Many of the features on modern aircraft like the A350 first saw the light of day on the super jumbo. The A380 introduced the widest economy seat, quietest cabin, freshest air, variable mood lighting and the ground-breaking inflight entertainment systems that have made flying so much more comfortable today.

With the A380 designed for long-haul flying, Airbus eased pilot workloads with new cockpit technology that built on its fly-by-wire systems. It added modular avionics, head-up displays, integrated the traffic avoidance and collision avoidance system into the autopilot and developed an automated brake and vacate feature for landing.

While the order book and production line have closed and despite the wreckage the pandemic has left behind, the A380 will not be disappearing any time soon. By June 2022, Emirates had around 60% of its A380s back in the air and the airline has said it expects to be flying the aircraft well into the 2030s.

Not every passenger wants to sit in an aircraft for 20 hours on a direct flight from Australia to London and many prefer what the super jumbo has to offer. When viewed in isolation the A380 may not have lived up to its financial objectives but it has changed the face of aviation, and its DNA lives on in those aircraft that have followed.

What's next?

Developing commercial aircraft is a little like creating a chain; would there be an A380 if the 747 was not developed first or would there be a 787 without an A350? What is illuminating is that when air travel restarted post-COVID-19, the airlines that had A380s soon got them out of the desert and back flying.

Flying from Sydney to Dallas nonstop is point to point and yet is an ideal A380 route, as is a peak period Shanghai to Beijing domestic flight. Carriers like Emirates, Qatar, Qantas, British Airways, United Airlines, Cathay Pacific, and Singapore Airlines have built their long-haul businesses on the backs of the 747 and the A380.

Only time will tell if the twin-engine, long-haul model of the 787 and A350 proves to be just a successful in the next 20 to 30 years as the big jets have been.

ABOVE • *The 747-8 Freighter launch customer Cargolux uses the new freighter's unique nose-door cargo loading capability.* BOEING

LEFT • *Hi Fly the Mirpuri Foundation campaign 'Save the Coral Reefs' by painting one of its A380 aircraft with a special-themed livery, aiming to reinforce worldwide the message of sustainability and protection of the seas.* BOEING

ABOVE RIGHT • *Airbus' 100th A380 was delivered to Malaysian Airlines, the last to join the carrier's A380 fleet.* EXMHGE

RIGHT • *Air France operated the first commercial A380 flight to Rio de Janeiro in 2016.* LUIS A NEVES

A Family Affair

Airbus and Boeing have been quick to develop aircraft families to meet operator needs and which respond adequately to market demand. Michael Doran looks at the design, comfort, and efficiency of these next generation aircraft.

The size and economics of the Boeing 747 brought air travel to the masses and cemented the concept that big was indeed better throughout the late 20th century. Airbus later sought to build on that with the A380.

The next step change came with the introduction of new generation widebodies, like the Boeing 787 Dreamliner and the Airbus A350 that switched the widebody model from hub and spoke to point to point services.

These aircraft, plus the Airbus A330neo and the yet to be introduced Boeing 777X, benefitted hugely from the new engine technology that reduced fuel burn, noise, and CO2 emissions.

Boeing 787 Dreamliner

While Boeing's 787 is officially known as the Dreamliner, it could just as easily be called the Gamechanger, because in so many ways it shifted widebody commercial aviation away from four-engine to twin-engine aircraft. It was the start of a shift away from the hub-and-spoke model, so suited to the 747 and A380, toward more efficient point to point routes.

Boeing first announced the new twin-engine programme in January 2003, dubbing it the 7E7, with many believing the 'E' represented efficiency or environmentally friendly. When the aircraft was officially designated as the 787, Boeing said the 'E' had always just stood for eight.

The 787 was launched in April 2004, with Japan's All Nippon Airways, placing an order for 50 aircraft. Boeing forecast ANA's first 787 would be delivered in 2008 but that was delayed until September 2011, with its first commercial flight in October from Hong Kong to Tokyo.

The 787 signalled a change in manufacturing philosophy at Boeing, with much of the design work subcontracted out to the manufacturers who would supply the aircraft components. By far the most well-known shift was the use of carbon fibre materials to reduce

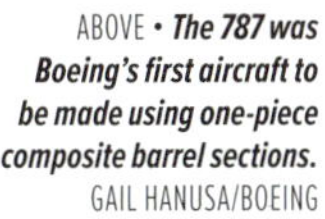

ABOVE • *The 787 was Boeing's first aircraft to be made using one-piece composite barrel sections.* GAIL HANUSA/BOEING

RIGHT • *JAL reconfigured its three-class 787 Dreamliner to have 161 passengers, giving all onboard extra comfort and space.* JAPAN AIRLINES

TOP RIGHT • *Etihad Airways A350-1000 at the Dubai Airshow 2021, one of 20 ordered by the airline.* AIRBUS - JEAN-VINCENT REYMONDON

weight, with around 50% (by weight) made up of composite materials.

Prior to the 787, commercial aircraft fuselages were typically made using aluminium sheets, held together by more than 50,000 fasteners. The 787 was the first to be made using one-piece composite barrel sections.

Adding to its next-generation features, the 787 would have new engines, a choice between the Rolls-Royce Trent 1000 or the General Electric GEnx, that would reduce fuel consumption and emissions by up to 15% when compared to previous types. While the new engines delivered on their performance, fuel burn and emission reduction targets, the Rolls-Royce engine suffered a string of entry-into-service issues that led to extensive groundings while solutions were developed.

Onboard issues and fires from the aircraft's battery systems also caused a grounding in 2013, but despite these significant setbacks the Dreamliner has become one of Boeing's best-selling and most popular commercial aircraft.

By April 2022, Boeing had delivered nearly 1,500 Dreamliners and has another 479 orders waiting to be filled. Major airline operators include All Nippon Airways, United Airlines, Japan Airlines, Etihad Airways and Qatar Airways.

In a two-class configuration, the 787-8 can carry 248 passengers 7,305nm (13,530km), the 787-9 296 passengers 7,565nm (14,010km) and the 787-10 336 passengers 6,330nm (11,730km).

The big strength of the 787 is turning long thin routes into viable markets, due to the lower operating costs and passenger appeal of the Dreamliner. Air New Zealand was the first customer for the 787-9 and uses it to good effect on routes from Auckland to New York, Chicago, and Los Angeles.

United Airlines has used the 787-9 on the 7,470nm Sydney-Houston route and the 7,339nm San Francisco-Singapore route. Qantas launched the first direct flights between Australia and the UK, with its Perth-London covering 7,829nm.

These 17+ hour flights are made bearable by the lower cabin altitude pressure, higher humidity levels, large windows, and LED mood lighting. The 787's internal cabin pressure is the equivalent of 6,000 feet with 15% humidity, compared to the typical 8,000 feet and 4% humidity on legacy aircraft.

The 787 is a delight for passengers to fly on and for airlines to operate, but there is no escaping from the entry-into-service issues and delays that beset its early days. In 2022, Boeing is unable to deliver newly manufactured 787s due to a fuselage manufacturing defect that Boeing is working with the US Federal Aviation Administration (FAA) to overcome.

ABOVE • *For those liking numerical symmetry, in 2020, Air France was the recipient of the 350th A350.* AIRBUS SAS 2019 ALEXANDRE DOUMENJOU - MASTER FILMS

LEFT • *The Trent 7000 from Rolls-Royce is the exclusive engine for the A330neos.* ROLLS-ROYCE

ABOVE • *The A330-200 is one of three variants of the original A330, now known as the A330ceo.* OMAN AIR

RIGHT • *Deliveries of the 777X from Boeing have been pushed back to 2025.* LUNCHWITHALENS/ FLICKR

BELOW • *The front fan of the GE9X engine which will power the 777X is as wide as the body of an entire Boeing 737.* TIM STAKE/BOEING

It is powered by two Rolls-Royce Trent XWB turbofan engines and the prototype completed its first flight on June 14, 2013. It gained type certification from the European Union Aviation Safety Agency (EASA) in September 2014 and from the FAA two months later.

The A350 broke new ground when EASA approved it for ETOPS 370 (extended-range twin-engine operations performance standards), allowing it to fly for more than six hours on one engine. It was the first airliner to be approved for ETOPS beyond 180 minutes before entry into service.

Airbus also had a significant win when it received regulatory approval for a Common Type Rating covering pilot training between the A350 XWB and the A330. Over time, Airbus built a successful strategy, particularly in Asia, of using the A330 and A350 in combination to develop routes and the flexibility of the common pilot rating proved attractive to airlines.

The A350-900 first customer delivery was to Qatar Airways in December 2014, and it entered service on January 15, 2015, operating from Doha to Frankfurt. Qatar also launched the A350-1000 on a February 24, 2018, flight from Doha to London.

As the A380 was staking its place in the market, the A350 was quickly winning new customers and marked a turning point at Airbus, which

Airbus A350

In 2005 Airbus was losing ground to Boeing in the twin-engine widebody market, where the new-generation B787 was proving attractive to airlines and passengers.

Starting in 2007, Airbus designed a new, clean slate carbon fibre reinforced polymer aircraft with two engines, the A350 XWB (eXtra Wide Body). The XWB designation came from a fuselage that is 12.7cm (5in) wider than the 787, at a seated passenger's eye level, although it is narrower than the 777 cabin.

The wider fuselage means the A350 can offer up to ten abreast seating, as does the 777, whereas the 787 typically offers nine seats per row. In a high-density layout the A350 has a maximum seating capacity of 440 to 475, depending on the variant.

In a nod to its European heritage, the A350 is produced from various sites across Europe, including the UK, Germany, France, and Spain.

shifted its focus away from the A380 to producing next-generation, twin-engine widebodies.

After Qatar had received the first four A350-900s, next in line were Vietnam Airlines, Finnair, Singapore Airlines, LATAM Airlines, and Ethiopian Airlines. In 2020, just seven years after its first flight, Airbus delivered its 350th A350, this one to Air France.

The stretched A350-1000 XWB was designed with a fuselage extended by 20ft (6m) which lifted maximum capacity to 480 passengers. Its increased maximum take-off weight (MTOW) and more powerful engines made it attractive for transpacific operators, such as Cathay Pacific, Singapore Airlines and United Airlines.

It also made the A350 a potent competitor to the Boeing 777-300ER, which was gaining orders as a replacement for aging B747s. The A350-1000 brought new customers and markets to Airbus, including British Airways, Virgin Atlantic and Japan Air Lines, the latter being the first Japanese operator of a next-generation twin-engine widebody from Airbus.

The -1000 also gained traction with 787 operators who saw the A350 as complementary to their next generation aircraft, with it becoming the go to aircraft for the world's longest airline routes.

These included the Singapore to San Francisco route of 7,350nm, operated by Singapore Airlines, Manilla to New York at 7,400nm operated by Philippine Airlines and Singapore to Los Angeles at 7,650nm by Singapore Airlines.

Singapore Airlines uses a specially configured A350-900 ULR (Ultra Long Range) aircraft on the 8,300nm Singapore to Newark (US) route. In May 2022, Australian airline Qantas confirmed its order for A350 -1000

aircraft for its flights connecting Sydney to London or New York non-stop.

The A350 was born at a time when giants ruled the airline world and is now reshaping how ultra-long-haul travel happens, with almost anywhere on the planet reachable with one flight. That's a lot to achieve within its first decade of flying.

Airbus A330neo

The Airbus A330-300, which shares its airframe with early variants of the A340, first flew in November 1992. It entered commercial service with French airline, Air Inter in January 1994

and the slightly shorter A330-200 variant followed in 1998.

After 20 successful years of service, the A330 was being overtaken by new generation widebodies, such as the Boeing 787 Dreamliner, with their more powerful, quieter, and fuel-efficient engines.

In 2014, Airbus announced the new A330neo (new engine option), which many wrongly assumed was the same aircraft with a new engine, which entered service with launch customer TAP Air Portugal in December 2018.

The original A330 came in three variants, the A330-200, A330-200F and

LEFT • *Singapore Airlines is the first to fly the new Boeing 787-10 Dreamliner, the newest and largest member of the Dreamliner family.* JOSHUA DRAKE/BOEING

LEFT • *In 2017, Boeing debuted the 787-10 Dreamliner, the third member of the 787 Dreamliner family.* BOEING

BELOW • *Colombian flag carrier Avianca was the recipient of Boeing's 500th 787 Dreamliner, a 787-8.* TIM STAKE/BOEING

Boeing 787-8/-9/-10 and 777X technical specifications

	787-8	787-9	787-10	777X
Length	57m (187ft)	63m (206ft 8in)	68m (22ft 1in)	76.73m (251ft 9in)
Height	17m (55ft 9in)	17m (5ft 9in)	17m (55ft 9in)	19.68m (64ft 7in)
Fuselage width	5.75m (18ft 10in)	5.77m (18ft 11in)	5.75m (18ft 10in)	6.2m (20ft 4in)
Wingspan	60m (196ft 10in)	60m (19ft 10in)	60m (196ft 10in)	71.75m (235ft 5in)
Passengers (max)	381	420	440	426 (2-class)
Cabin length	51m (167ft 4in)	56m (183ft 9in)	62m (203ft 5in)	N/A
Max cabin width	5.49m (18ft)	5.49m (18ft)	5.49m (18ft)	5.96m (19ft 7in)
Cabin Height	2.5m (8ft 2in)	2.5m (8ft 2in)	2.5m (8ft 2in)	N/A
Max take-off weight	227 tonnes (502,500lb)	254 tonnes (559,993lb)	254 tonnes (559,993lb)	351.5 tonnes (775,000lb)
Max landing weight	172 tonnes (380,000lb)	192 tonnes (424,994lb)	201 tonnes (444,994lb)	180 tonnes (775,000lb)
Max zero fuel weight	161 tonnes (355,500lb)	181 tonnes (400,000lb)	193 tonnes (425,000lb)	180 tonnes (400,000lb)
Max fuel capacity	126,917 lit (33,528 US gal)	126,425 lit (33,398 US gal)	126,429 lit (33,399 US gal)	197,700 lit (52,300 US gal)
Engines	2 x GEnx-1B / Trent 1000 (2 x 64,000lbf)	2 x GEnx-1B / Trent 1000 (2 x 71,000lbf)	2 x GEnx-1B / Trent 1000 (2 x 76,000lbf)	2 x General Electric GE9X-105B1A (2 x 110,000lbf)
Typical cruise speed	M.077	M.078	M.077	N/A
Max flight level	43,000ft	43,100ft	43,000ft	43,100ft

Source: Boeing

A330-300, and is now referred to as the A330ceo (current engine option). It had three engine options, the Rolls-Royce Trent 700, Pratt & Whitney PW4000 and the General Electric CF6.

However, Airbus opted to have the Rolls-Royce Trent 7000 as the exclusive choice of powerplant on both the A330-800neo and the A330-900neo.

The Trent 7000 is not just an upgraded Trent 700, but a new engine that combines the sustainable credentials of the latest generation Roll-Royce Trent XWB, the engine on the Airbus A350. The 7000 gives the A330 a step change in performance, most noticeably a 14% better fuel burn, which delivers significant reduction in emissions and operating costs.

Its larger fan, 112-in (285cm) diameter compared to 97in (246cm) on the 700, moves greater volumes of air at lower speeds, making it quieter and well below international noise standards. The 7000 is also fully compliant with using sustainable aviation fuel (SAF), adding further to the A330neo's green credentials.

Beyond the new engines, the A330neo benefits from a new set of wings that give it the highest wingspan and aspect ratio for any widebody airliner in its category. This greater aspect ratio lowers induced drag and gives higher lift at all stages of flight, leading to lower fuel burn and CO2 emissions.

The new wing, in common with the A350, incorporates swept back wing tips, which are part of the wing structure and not distinct parts added on. The carbon fibre winglets on the A330neo are seamlessly integrated with the horizontally extended outer span wing section and together they extend the aircraft's overall wingspan to 64m (70 yards) compared to 60.3m on the A330ceo.

Three-dimensional computational fluid dynamics (CFD) tools have shaped the wing twist, which ensures that the airflow is optimised at every point along the span from root to tip, even as the wing slightly rotates while naturally flexing in flight.

RIGHT • *ANA continues to show faith in the Dreamliner family. In 2026, it took delivery of its 50th 787 Dreamliner, and has recently committed to more 787s, four 787-9 jets and five options replacing previous domestic 777 models that are slated for retirement.*
TIM STAKE/BOEING

RIGHT • *Airbus' Airspace Explorer – a specially configured A350-900ULR flight test aircraft fitted with the company's award-winning Airspace cabin – is exhibited at the ILA Berlin air show 2022.*
AIRBUS/MAX_LEITMEIER-SCHWARZBILD

Airbus A350/-1000, A330neo technical specifications

	A350	A350-1000	A330-800	A330-900
Length	66.80m (219.2ft)	73.79m (242.1ft)	58.36m (191ft.47in)	63.69m (208ft.96in)
Height	17.05m (55.11ft)	17.08m (56ft)	17.39m (57.1ft)	16.79m (55.1ft)
Fuselage width	5.96m (19.7ft)	5.96m (19.7ft)	5.64m (18.6ft)	5.64m (18.6ft)
Wingspan	64.75m (212.5ft)	64.75m (212.5ft)	64m (210ft)	64m (210ft)
Passengers (max)	440	480	406	460
Cabin length	51.04m (167.5 1ft)	58.03m (190.5ft)	45m (147.64ft)	50.36m (165.3ft)
Max cabin width	5.61m (18.5ft)	5.61m (18.5ft)	5.26m (17.26ft)	5.26m (27.3ft)
Cabin Height	N/A	2.2m (7.22ft)	N/A	N/A
Max take-off weight	280 tonnes (617,300lb)	319 tonnes (705,300lb)	250 tonnes (553,002lb)	251 tonnes (553,400lb)
Max landing weight	207 tonnes (456,400lb)	236 tonnes 520,300lb)	186 tonnes (410,056lb)	191 tonnes (421,0008lb)
Max zero fuel weight	195.7 tonnes (431,400lb)	223 tonnes (491,600lb)	N/A	181 tonnes (399,000lb)
Max fuel capacity	141,000 lit (37,248 US gal)	159,000 lit (42,003 US gal)	139,076 lit (139,740 US gal)	139,090 lit (36,750 US gal)
Engines	2 x Rolls Royce Trent XWB (2 x 94,900lbf)	2 x Rolls Royce Trent XWB (2 x 94,900lbf)	2x Rolls-Royce Trent 7000-72 Turbofan (2 x 72,834lbf)	2x Rolls-Royce Trent 7000-72 Turbofan (2 x 72,834lbf)
Typical cruise speed	M.089	M.089	M.074	M.086
Max flight level	43,100ft	43,100ft	41,450ft	41,450ft

Source: Airbus

The A330-900 is proving the popular choice, with its range of 7,200nm (13,334km) and eight-abreast seating up to a maximum of 460 passengers, or a more comfortable 260-300 in a three-class layout.

The 16ft (4.8m) shorter A330-800's range is 8,150nm (15,094km) and can seat up to 406, or 220-260 in a three-class configuration. Both variants have a MTOW of 251 tonnes (553,000lb) and a maximum speed of 496kts (918kph).

As of April 2025, there were seven A330-800neos and 148 A330-900neos in service, with airlines including TAP Air Portugal, Delta Air Lines and Azul Brazilian Airlines. In contrast there are 1,269 A330ceos operating, split almost evenly between the A330-200 and A330-300 variants.

Given that the A330neo only entered service in late 2018, in aircraft terms it

ABOVE LEFT • *Air Senegal was the first African airline to receive and operate the newest member of the A330 family. Fitted with a three-class cabin and 290 seats, it helped launch the airline's Dakar-Paris route.* AIRBUS SAS 2019 PHILIPPE MASCLET · MASTER FILMS

ABOVE RIGHT • *The 777X will feature an enhanced cabin environment including lower cabin noise, and improved temperature control. Advanced LED lighting is available throughout the aircraft such as the gallery area in business class.* BOEING

LEFT • *The external look of the 787 Dreamliner was revealed in 2015.* BOEING

ABOVE • *Broadcast live via satellite worldwide and webcast, the 787 Dreamliner was unveiled during a one-hour ceremony at its Everett, Washington., final assembly facility.* BOEING

RIGHT • *Singapore Airlines reintroduced flights to New York with the introduction of its A350 900ULR aircraft.* AIRBUS SAS 2018 PHILIPPE MASCLET - MASTER FILMS

Guinness World Record attempt in 2017 saw the GE9X deliver 134,300lb, taking the record for the world's most powerful commercial jet engine.

According to Boeing, the combination of the new wing, next-generation GE9X engine and other fuel-efficient methods will give a 10% reduction in fuel burn, emissions, and operating costs than its competition.

Passengers will enjoy the new cabin, which will feature the same comfort and wellbeing features as on the 787 Dreamliner. Thinner interior walls and better insulation give the 777X a four inch (10cm) wider cabin than the 777-300, making room for 18in (46cm) seats in a ten-abreast configuration.

The development of the 777X and the GE9X have not gone entirely to plan, with a number of delays including changes in its development, test pauses, and ongoing work stoppages, pushing the first delivery back until at least 2026.

Beset with production issues on the 787 and certification delays on the 777X, with type certification now expected in late 2025 or early 2026, in 2022 Boeing took the unexpected decision to pause production of the 777X, only reinstating its Everett assembly line in the last quarter of 2023. It now forecasts that first deliveries will commence in 2026, seven years later than announced when launching the aircraft, with Lufthansa confirmed as the launch customer.

At the end of April 2025, Boeing reported it had orders for 580 777s. Major customers listed include Emirates (262 aircraft), Qatar Airways (94), Singapore Airlines (31), Etihad Airways (25), Lufthansa (27), Cathay Pacific (21) and Korean Air (20).

Given the long delays, it is likely some of those orders will not be delivered, perhaps to be replaced with 787s or Airbus A350s. At this stage, the 777X shows a lot of promise, particularly to the many 777-300ER operators with ageing aircraft, but it is up to Boeing to ensure that promise is delivered.

is still relatively young. How well it fares in the future will be impacted by the emerging trend to narrowbody long-haul with aircraft such as the A321neo LR/XLR and the success of the Boeing 777X when it arrives.

Boeing 777X

Following the introduction of the Boeing 787 and the Airbus A350 and A330neo, the Boeing 777 was starting to look a little outdated and tired, despite its decades of success. The cockpit technology, new cabins and fuel and emission reducing engines available on new generation widebodies were leaving the 777 behind.

Boeing knew the 777 needed to be upgraded if it was to maintain its place in the market, and in 2013 it launched two variants of the new 777X aircraft, the 777-8 and the 777-9. It is the largest twin-engine jet in the world and with a length of 251ft (76.7m) the 777-9 is nine feet (2.8m) longer than the popular 777-300ER.

That extra length allows the 777-9 to carry up to 426 passengers 7,285nm (13,500km) while its smaller cousin, the 777-8 can take 384 to a range of 8,730nm (16,170km). The current

777-300ER has a range of 7,370nm (13,649km) with up to 396 passengers.

Like the A330neo, the 777X has a new carbon fibre-reinforced polymer wing, which is so wide it needs folding wingtips to fit into a normal size airport parking bay. When on the ground with the tips folded, the wingspan is 212ft 8in (64.82m) and in the air that extends to 235ft 5in (71.75m).

Efficiency and power will come from the General Electric GE9X, a new high bypass turbofan developed exclusively for the 777X. The GE9X is the largest and most powerful commercial aircraft engine built, with a massive 132in (335cm) fan. While General Electric list the engine's thrust at 105,000lb, a

RIGHT • *Delta is replacing its ageing 767-300ERs with Airbus A330-900s on its transpacific routes.* AIRBUS - MASTER FILMS - JEAN-BAPTISTE ACCARIEZ

Battlegrounds in the Sky

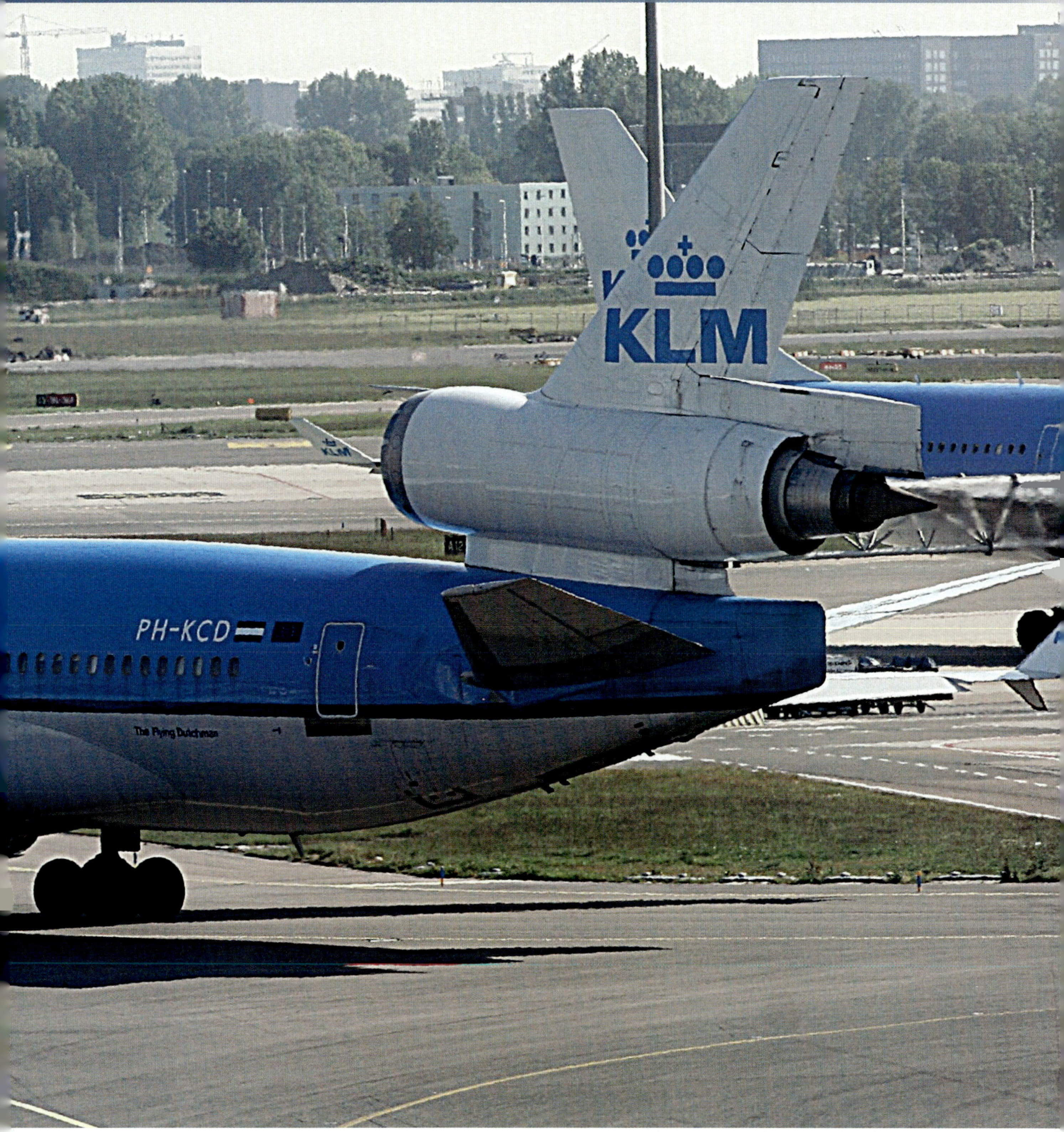

ABOVE • *In 2014, the curtain came down on commercial passenger operations for the MD-11 as KLM retired its last jet (not pictured) having flown from Montreal to Amsterdam.* IAN GRATTON

The might of the duopoly that is Airbus and Boeing in the widebody market has rarely been seriously threatened, but that hasn't stopped some from entering the fray.

Long before the emergence of Airbus, McDonnell Douglas led the competition to Boeing. Launched in 1986, the McDonnell Douglas MD-11 is a medium to long range widebody jet airliner, which arose out of the development of the DC-10.

Despite a number of technical innovations, already discussed in a previous chapter, the aircraft suffered issues with its flight control system, wherein the flap lever between the two pilots could accidentally be dislodged. The problem was finally resolved in 1992.

In addition to the passenger variant, the MD-11P, which was produced from 1988 to 1998, it was with cargo operations that the aircraft found greater service.

In 1986, the MD-11C (Combi) was introduced and picked up exclusively by Alitalia. Cargo could be carried alongside passengers on the main deck, which had a rear cargo door

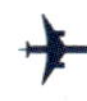

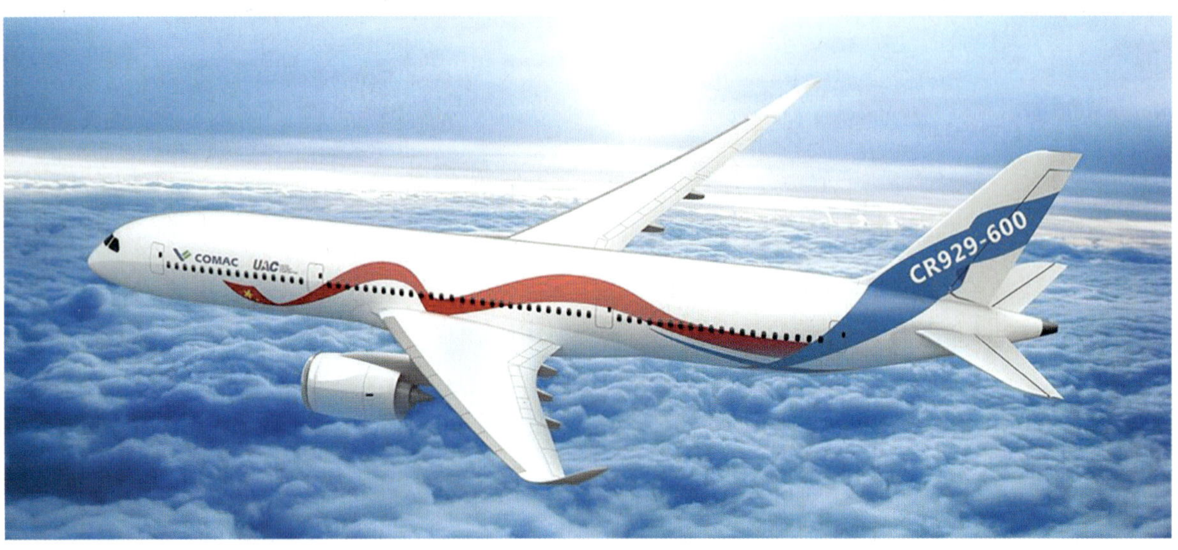

LEFT • *A rendering of the CR929 from COMAC. Following delays, it is hoped this Sino-Russian joint venture will prove competition to both Airbus and Boeing.* CRAIC

RIGHT • *Cubana, the national carrier of Cuba, is the last operator of passenger services on the Il-96-300 and was the first outside Russia to order and receive the aircraft.* TONY HISGETT

and room for up to 10 pallets of cargo, as well as in the belly of the aircraft. The Combi could also be configured to an all-passenger main deck.

Just five Combis were produced, and all were subsequently converted to full freighters.

The MD-11CF (Convertible Freighter) was launched in 1991 following an order received from Martinair for three aircraft plus two options. The CF included a large forward port side cargo door for the main deck between the passenger doors, the aircraft could be used in all-passenger or all-freighter configuration.

The MD-11F freighter version was the second version of the MD-11 produced. It was first put on offer in 1986. This was also the last version of the type to be produced due to poor sales.

BELOW • *The Il-86 kickstarted Russia's widebody aircraft programme.* DICK GILBERT

For this type there where two main customers, FedEx taking 22 aircraft and Lufthansa taking 14 aircraft.

Lufthansa Cargo took delivery of its first two MD-11 freighters (former registrations D-ALCA and D-ALCB) in June 1998, followed by the third aircraft in August of the same year and given the registration D-ALCC. In total, Lufthansa Cargo operated 19 MD-11, including the last ever manufactured (former registration D-ALCN, serial number 48806, delivered January 25, 2001) and the last ever delivered (former registration D-ALCM, serial number 48805, delivered February 22, 2001) aircraft of this type.

The MD-11 freighter is 61.4m long with a wingspan of 51.7m and a height of up to 18m. It has a cargo capacity of up to 94.7 tons, divided into 26 positions on the main deck and up to 14 more on the lower deck. Lufthansa Cargo's freighters were powered by three General Electric CF6-80C2D1F jet engines, each with 273.57 kN standard thrust. The maximum take-off weight (MTOW) was 285.99 metric tons, resulting in a range of 7,242km.

On Sunday October 17, 2021, a Lufthansa Cargo MD-11 landed at Frankfurt Airport for the last time, marking the end of commercial service of the three-engine MD-11F aircraft type at Lufthansa Cargo after more than 23 years. The aircraft with registration D-ALCC, also the last MD-11F registered in Europe, was sold to an American cargo airline.

"We are very grateful to our MD-11F fleet for over two decades of loyal service. We know that this particular aircraft has an incredible number of fans, throughout our colleagues at Lufthansa as well as among aviation enthusiasts worldwide. The decisive factor for the introduction of the MD-11F at Lufthansa Cargo in the late nineties was its significantly better fuel efficiency compared to the widebody freighter previously used. In the future, we will rely on the twin-engine Boeing 777F for the same reason," said Dorothea von Boxberg, chairperson of the executive board and CEO of Lufthansa Cargo.

Since November 2013, Lufthansa Cargo has been gradually replacing the MD-11F freighters with twin-engine Boeing 777 freighters, which are much quieter and operate with lower emissions.

Slow sales and wider unfavourable economics have tended to force the hand of manufacturers, leading to the

ABOVE • In 2014, Aeroflot retired the final Il-96 from its fleet.
COLIN COOKE, FLICKR

LEFT • A sorry state. An Il-96 stands parked after serving with Aeroflot.
ALAN WILSON

BELOW • Only three of the enlarged Il-96-400T entered service for cargo operations.
COLIN COOKE PHOTO

ending of production and for some, Lockheed, to withdraw from the commercial aircraft market entirely. While some proposed new aircraft have never left the drawing boards, others have made the transition to market.

Sino-Russian collaboration

In 2012, PJSC UAC (United Aircraft Corporation) of Russia and China's COMAC formed a joint venture, CRAIC to explore the possibility of establishing a family of long-range, widebody commercial aircraft. However, UAC has subsequently been dropped from the programme, with COMAC confirming it was independently developing the aircraft.

Various Memorandum of Understandings (MoUs) later, the aircraft family was officially named in 2017 as CR929 (C-China, R-Russia). Following a breakdown in relations,

Russian participation in the programme has ceased with COMAC renaming the aircraft C929. Initially aimed towards the Chinese, Russian and Commonwealth of Independent States (CIS) markets, the twin aisle baseline version, the C929–600, will offer a three-class layout capable of carrying 280 passengers up to 12,000km. The family will be modified to include a shortened version, the C929–500 carrying 250 passengers up to 14,000km, and the stretched version C929–700 with a capacity of 320 passengers and a range up to 10,000km.

In 2018, Italy's Leonardo signed a MoU with Kangde Investment Group of China to establish a joint venture, Kangde Marco Polo Aerostructures Jiangsu Co. Ltd., for the development, production, and assembly of composite materials components for the C929 aircraft.

It is proposed that approximately 50% of the airframe structure will be comprised of new composite materials.

According to Alessandro Profumo, Leonardo's CEO, "Leonardo's decision to participate in the C929 provides further recognition of our advanced capabilities in the design and manufacture of composite aerostructures."

When held up against its main competitors, the Boeing 787 and Airbus A350, COMAC has set out basic requirements for the C929 of achieving a 10-15% advantage regarding operating expenses per seat; a required 15-18% advantage regarding fuel efficiency per seat and offer the best comfort thanks to a wider fuselage. It is also envisioned that the aircraft will offer a choice of two power plants from two suppliers. The C929 high-aspect-ratio wing will also feature sharklets to minimise drag and optimise fuel-burn.

The public got its first glance at what the cabin could look like during the 12th China International Aviation & Aerospace Exhibition in November 2018. A full-sized mock-up showed a three class LOPA: first-class, business-class and economy-class, as well as the C929 flight deck. The cabin was equipped with two rows of first-class, three rows of business-class, and four rows of economy-class. Also on display were an inflight entertainment system and the distinctive interior décor reflecting both Chinese and Russian styles.

Significant delays caused by disagreements involving suppliers and between both China and Russia have pushed back the entry date from 2024 to 2028 or even 2029.

COMAC has set an ambitious target of achieving 1,000 C929 sales between 2023 to 2045, and with these disagreements now apparently behind it, the venture will be hopeful of attracting firm interest. However, while Chinese airlines could be expected to follow party lines and place orders for the new aircraft, an international market remains to be convinced.

Russia's Design Bureau

Russia's widebody aircraft programme had been looking forward with the C929, the Soviet-era influence looms large. Worsening relations with the West are nothing new for UAC, who two years ago announced the proposed Il-96-400M as a direct and viable alternative to the Airbus A330-300 and Boeing 777-200.

The Il-96-400M is the latest member of Ilyushin Il-86/Il-96 family. In development since the early 2010s, the aircraft can carry 400 passengers in a single class configuration, powered by four Aviadvigatel PS-90A1 engines, each with a thrust of 38,360lb. At the beginning of 2022, Russian media reported that the Ministry of Industry and Trade expected the Il-96-400M to make its first flight by the end of the year.

Deputy Minister Oleg Bocharov, in a meeting with Prime Minister Mikhail Mishustin, was reported to comment that: "We plan that the Il-96-400M will make its first flight by the end of the year. It has expanded capabilities due to the lengthening of the fuselage and the use of design solutions for installing advanced engines."

Compared to the Il-96-300, the fuselage of the -400M has been lengthened by 9.35m and includes a modernised digital flight and navigation system. The deputy minister confirmed that the aircraft would be used as a flying laboratory for testing Aviadvigatel's PD-35 family of engines which have a thrust of 24 to 50 tons.

With no civilian customer on its books, plans to transfer Russian air command posts to the Il-96-400M were publicised in 2020, following completion of the aircraft's slipway assembly. The Russian Aerospace Force is reportedly set to receive two such 'Doomsday' aircraft in total, with a possible third ordered as required.

The Il-96-400M is an upgraded version of the first Il-96 aircraft, a four-engine long-range jet built by the Ilyushin Design Bureau, featuring supercritical wings fitted with winglets, a glass cockpit, and a fly-by-wire control system.

The aircraft is equipped with four PS-90A1 turbofan engines manufactured by Perm Motors Holding (Russia) attached

RIGHT • A collection of Il-96 and a solitary Il-86 aircraft parked in the storage area of Moscow Domodedovo Airport. ALAN WILSON

BELOW • An Il-96-300 operated by Russia State Transport, which operated VIP flights. MARKUS EIGENHEER

to underwing pylons. The engines feature high bypass and compression ratio resulting in improved aircraft flight performance. The Auxiliary Power Units are VSU-10-02, manufactured by Baranov Manufacturing Union (Omsk, Russia).

Russian airline Aeroflot was the first commercial operator of the Il-96 aircraft in 1992. From 1993 to 2014, the Russian flag carrier operated a fleet of six Il-96-300s until their retirement due to the jet's poor economics. In 2005, malfunctions in the jets' braking systems grounded the aircraft, while during a visit to Finland earlier that year, an unspecified mechanical malfunction on President Putin's Il-96, caused the Russian leader to use a back-up aircraft.

Production of the passenger version eventually ceased in 2009, with just a cargo variant continuing to be built. At the time production ended, a total of 21 Ilyushin Il-96 airliners were in service. In addition to Aeroflot, Ilyushin Design Bureau, KrasAir, Polet and Rossiya and an unspecified Russian airline were operating the aircraft. Currently, Cuba's national airline, Cubana de Aviación is the only remaining commercial operator of the Il-96-300, with two in active service, having been the first airline outside Russia to operate the type following a US$100m order in 2004. Cuban aircraft are configured for 262 passengers - 18 business-class seats with a 54in pitch and 244 in economy with 32in pitch. During the COVID-19 pandemic, the aircraft were used on charter flights between Mexico City and Havana to transfer Cuban and Mexican residents, who had not been able to return to their homes.

The Russian version offered a three-class passenger cabin layout accommodating 172 seats, two-class layout with 262 seats, or a single-class layout of 330 seats. In business-class, passengers enjoyed individual seat-back screens offering four channels for films, flight map, special information and forward view observation. Economy-class passengers had overhead monitors. A passenger satellite communication system allowed up to four passengers to make calls for a proscribed duration.

In the cockpit, the Il-96-300 aircraft is piloted by three crew members and kitted out with Russian-made avionics which includes six multifunctional colour-LCD displays (EFIS), Flight Management System (FMS), Inertial Navigation System, Collision air avoidance System (CAS) including mode 'S' transponder, EGPWS system, VHF communications and equipment permitting flights in RVSM conditions. The avionics package also includes the Mark V enhanced ground proximity warning system EGPWS from Honeywell Aerospace as well as the company's TCAS (CAS-100) and weather radar system (RDR-4B).

The other passenger variant is the Il-96M which was designed to be operated by a crew of two, eliminating the need for a flight engineer. With a range of 10,000km, it has a passenger capacity of 436. The Il-96M is based on the Il-96-300, but with a stretched fuselage and is 15 tonnes heavier. It can carry 321 passengers up to 10,400km, powered by Pratt & Whitney PW 2337 engines with a thrust rating of 165kN (37,000lb).

TOP • *A Varig MD-11 at Zurich Airport.*
COLIN COOKE PHOTO

ABOVE • *An Armenian Airlines Il-86 approaches Gatwick Airport.*
ALEX RANKIN

Il-86, Il-96-300, Il-96M and Il-96-400 selected specifications

	Il-86	Il-96-300	Il-96M	Il-96-400
Length	59.40m (194ft 11in)	55.35m (181ft.7in)	60.11m (197ft 3in)	63.94m (209ft 64in)
Height	15.80m (51ft 10in)	17.55m (57ft 7in)	17.55m (57ft 7in)	17.55m (57ft 7in)
Fuselage width	6.08m (19ft 11in)	6.08m (19ft 11in)	6.08m (19ft 11in)	6.08m (19ft 11in)
Wingspan	48m (157ft 6in)	60.1m (197ft 3in)	64.7m (212ft 3in)	60.1m (197ft 3in)
Passengers (max)	320	300	300	402
Engines	4x Kuznetsov NK-86	4 x Perm/Aviadvigatel PS-90A (4 x 35,100lbf)	4 x Pratt & Whitney PW2037 (4 x 38,25lbf)	4 x Perm/Aviadvigatel PS-90A1 (4 x 38,326lbf)
Typical cruise speed	M.078	M0.78	M0.78	M0.78
Max flight level	32,800ft	39,000ft	39,000ft	43,000ft

Source: Ilyushin

ABOVE • *A Finnair MD-11.*
AERO ICARUS

RIGHT • *After an eventful life, this Sabena MD-11 was eventually scrapped in 2018.* AERO ICARUS

The Il-96 is based on the Soviet-era Il-86 (NATO codename *Camber*) a four-engine medium-range jet airliner, with a capacity of 320 passengers, and the pioneer of Russia's widebody programme.

Work on the aircraft began in 1974, with the first prototype making its maiden flight in December 1976. Production began in October 1977, with launch customer Aeroflot receiving its first aircraft in September 1979. The Russian flag carrier had hoped to take advantage of the patriotic zeal surrounding the 1980 Moscow Summer Olympics to launch domestic services, but final tests and certification pushed back entry into service to December. International services followed six months later in July 1981.

Avionics on the Il-86 included a Pizhma-1 navigational system, GPS transceivers, a traffic collision avoidance system, an instrument landing system, a weather radar, a VOR radio and distance measuring equipment. A VSU-10 auxiliary power unit supplies power to the cabin.

The Il-86 was powered by four Kuznetsov NK-86 bypass turbojet engines, each generating 127.5kN of thrust. The NK-86 is an advanced version of the Kuznetsov NK-8. Produced by Kuznetsov Design Bureau, the engine is equipped with five-stage low-pressure compressors, six-stage high-pressure compressors, annular combustor cans, a single-stage high-pressure turbine, a dual-stage low-pressure turbine, engine pylons, thrust reversers and an electronic control system.

Despite the hopes and ambitions of the Russian government, the aircraft failed to live up to expectation. Production ended in 1993 after the completion of some 20 aircraft.

While many thought the days of the Il-86 and Il-96 aircraft were way behind us, a surprise announcement has reactivated the aircraft into service. During a Federation Council committee meeting on economic policy in March 2022, Russian Transportation Minister Vitaly Savelyev confirmed that S7, a oneworld Alliance member, would begin operations of two Il-96 and three Il-86 cargo airplanes.

"Now S7, under my patronage will adapt them, and we will fly," Savelyev is reported as saying.

As yet, there is no word on the passenger variant taking to the skies once more.

In service

Airlines continue to invest in new widebody aircraft and refurbishment of existing fleets, giving passengers a range of options for their long-haul travels.

ABOVE • *Between 2022 and 2027, the Lufthansa Group will receive a total of 32 Boeing Dreamliners.*
LUFTHANSA

According to Boeing: "passengers typically prefer the convenience of nonstop flights, and as regulation of airline service in international markets has relaxed, long-haul markets have become increasingly fragmented. New, more efficient widebody airplanes serve an increasing number of long-haul city pairs. This rising market fragmentation is boosting demand for smaller widebody passenger airplanes.

"Even as smaller widebody airplanes open new nonstop markets to service, the large end of the widebody market remains important. New, efficient, larger widebody airplanes find application in markets where there is very high demand for travel, where premium service is paramount, where global super connector airlines operate, where airports are especially congested and where there are airspace constraints."

Boeing's production woes

Writing in its 2024 annual report, Boeing acknowledged it was experiencing supply chain disruptions as a result of production quality issues, global supply chain constraints, and labour instability. The airframer says it is continuing to monitor the health and stability of the supply chain, which has led to a reduction in overall productivity.

During 2024, Boeing delivered 348 commercial airlines and had a backlog of over, 5,500 airplanes valued at $435bn. Orders during the year included 30 787-9 airplanes for flydubai.

The 787 programme exited the year at a production rate of five per month and has plans to expand South Carolina operations. In January 2025, the 777X programme resumed FAA certification flight testing, and the company still anticipates first delivery of the 777-9 in 2026.

In the report, the company noted it was "following the lead of the FAA as we work through the certification process, and the FAA will ultimately determine the timing of certification and entry into service. There have been delays on each of these development programmes and if we experience additional delays in achieving certification, our financial position, results of operations and cash flows would be adversely impacted.

"A number of our customers have contractual remedies, including compensation for late deliveries or rights to reject individual airplane deliveries based on delivery delays. Delays on the 737, 777X and 787 programmes have resulted in, and may continue to result in, customers having the right to terminate orders, be compensated for late deliveries and/or substitute orders for other Boeing aircraft."

Keeping the faith

Customers to have ordered the 787 include United Airlines, who in 2023, announced plans which would make it the world's largest 787 operator, exercising options to order 50 787-9s and securing an additional 50 options, bringing its order book to 15 firm orders. Deliveries will begin in 2028 and last until 2031. The move is designed to allow United to simplify its international fleet.

In Latin America, LATAM is investing in having one of the most modern fleets in the region. It's currently the largest 787 operator, a position reinforced by its announcement to purchase 10 787s with options for five more. LATAM currently operates 37 787-8s and 787-9s and, including its latest order, expects to grow the fleet to 52 Dreamliners by 2030. The 787 enables the airline to maximise capacity on popular routes and launch new routes including its nonstop flight to Sydney, Australia.

Retrofit focus

Following 18 months of research, 2,500 hours of customer testing and 184 days in Singapore, Air New Zealand's very first retrofitted Boeing 787-9 Dreamliner welcomed passengers on board for the first time in mid-May, 2025.

The aircraft, ZK-NZH, is the first in the airline's 787–9 fleet to undergo a world-first, full nose-to-tail retrofit. The scope of the retrofit includes new seats in every cabin, including the new Business Premier Luxe seats in the Business Premier cabin, new carpet throughout the aircraft, new curtains between cabins and galleys, new wallpaper, hands-free waste disposal, and amenity holders in the lavatories, Sky Pantry installed in the Economy cabin and new inflight entertainment screens and system.

The aircraft LOPA (Layout of Passenger Accommodation) on all 14 aircraft will be reconfigured to have 272 seats: featuring four Business Premier Luxe seats, 22 Business Premier seats, 33 Premium Economy seats, and 213 Economy seats, including 13 Economy Skycouch.

Currently, the airline's 787-9 aircraft have two different LOPA or configurations: nine aircraft with 302 seats, and five aircraft with 275 seats.

All 14 Boeing 787-9s will be updated to the new cabin layout by the end of 2026.

Digital native airline

In the Middle East, Saudi Arabia's General Authority of Civil Aviation (GACA) has officially granted an Air Operator's Certificate (AOC) to Riyadh Air, authorising the airline to start commercial flight operations. The airline was launched in 2023 by the Public Investment Fund (PIF) and will operate a fleet of 72 Boeing 787-9 Dreamliner airplanes, with the first commercial flight due in late 2025.

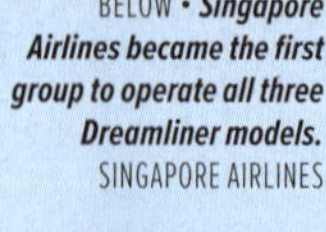

BELOW • *Singapore Airlines became the first group to operate all three Dreamliner models.*
SINGAPORE AIRLINES

ABOVE • *Uganda Airlines chose the A330neo as its very first Airbus aircraft.*
AIRBUS – JEAN-VINCENT REYMONDON

Riyadh Air's Boeing 787-9 fleet configuration will accommodate 290 guests: Business Elite (four seats) and 24 in Business, both in a 1-2-1 fully flat-bed layout using the bespoke Safran Unity seat with a length of 78in and a width of 22.5in, all featuring 52in-high walls and sliding privacy doors along with adjustable privacy dividers between centre seats.

Premium Economy accommodates 39 seats in a 2-3-2 layout with a seat pitch of 38in and width of 19.2in, while Economy will have 223 seats in a 3-3-3 layout with a 31in pitch and width of 17.2in.

The cabins feature some of the largest touchscreens in the air, all featuring 4K OLED technology, including 32in monitors in Business Elite, 22in in business-class, 15.6in in Premium Economy, and 13.3in in Economy.

Additionally, Business Elite features a double bed in the centre front seats while all seats in Business Elite and Business feature A/C power and two USB-C and one USB-A charging points. Premium Economy passengers will have privacy head wings, increased seat storage, versatile and expandable side table

design, refined recliner lounge comfort with calf rest and four USB-C charging points, while the signature theme of all cabins is a distinctive canopy twist design that evokes the elegance of traditional Arabic tents. Economy will have six-way adjustable headrests and two USB-C charging points.

According to the airline, Mocha Gold and veined stone accents in premium cabins offer a subtle, elegant contrast to rich purple textures. A thoughtfully curated palette: dark indigo, mocha, iridescent tones, skyline blue, sunset peach, and lavender, evoke a rich sophistication, seamlessly weaving the identity of the city of Riyadh into a modern expression of luxury felt throughout every cabin.

As a digitally native airline, Riyadh Air loyalty members will enjoy Viasat's seamless, free onboard streaming, social scrolling, web browsing, and gaming onboard, available from gate to gate (where permitted). Customers who sign up for the airline's loyalty scheme will receive free Wi-Fi. Viasat's network will enable live TV on the aircraft's seatback screens, providing a variety of news and sports channels.

Collaborating with Devialet, the high-end French audio technology company's acoustic technology will be integrated directly into Business Elite and Business class headrests, delivering immersive, high-fidelity sound without the need for headphones.

The carrier will also be the first airline to launch Panasonic Avionics' fully integrated IFE interactive design and publishing tool - Modular Interactive (MI), a full-featured interactive design tool which offers a quick and easy way to respond to the latest guest trends and provide seasonal updates and promotions.

Airbus takes consistent approach

Airbus delivered 766 commercial aircraft to 86 customers around the world in 2024, including 32 examples of its A330 family and 57 from its A350 family.

LEFT • *Air New Zealand's retrofitted 787-9 fleet will feature new Business Premier Luxe seats at the front of the aircraft, which offer more space and an upgraded experience from the airline's baseline, lie-flat, business-class accommodations.* AIR NEW ZEALAND

As Christian Scherer, the CEO of commercial aircraft at Airbus noted: "2024 confirmed sustained demand for new aircraft. We won key customer decisions with most important customers and saw phenomenal momentum for our widebody orderbook, complementing our leading position in the single aisle market. On deliveries, we kept our trajectory and celebrated several landmark firsts. These include the first ever A321XLR as well as first A330neo and A350 deliveries to several customers globally."

In 2024, Airbus used the occasion of that year's Aircraft Interiors Expo (AIX) to reveal a special A330neo full-size mock-up, showing the company's proposed new 'Airspace' cabin features. These include a new customisable mood lighting feature, a new welcome panel, new linings for the interior sidewall, ceiling and door frame panels, as well as electro-dimmable windows (EDWs). These new features will become available for customers from 2027/2028.

The enhanced ceiling lighting at Doors-2 called Airspace Welcome Panel, featuring the company's stencil pattern, will be standard in all new A330neos delivered from Q1 2026. Furthermore, Airbus will offer as an option the possibility for airlines to customise it.

A new lighting option which Airbus has christened Airspace Hero Light will be introduced as a premium product for the A330neo in 2027. This will be a key differentiation opportunity for an airline in the Doors-1 to Doors-2 area, being customisable with 16m colours and a unique pattern. It is typically the business class section where there is no middle

BELOW • *LATAM is the currently the largest 787 operator in Latin America.* LATAM

set of overhead bins attached to the ceiling as the Airspace lateral bins provide sufficient storage capacity.

The new sidewall will have the design language consistent with A350 and A320 Family's Airspace cabins. Passengers will also benefit from additional comfort since the new sidewalls offer 5mm extra shoulder clearance at every window seat, as well as 50mm more foot-space — thanks to the re-profiled dado panel at the floor level. Overall, the new sidewall and dado panels' industrial solution would save approximately 85kg throughout the aircraft according to Airbus engineering estimates. Meanwhile, the new matching ceiling panels are also

lighter than the previous design — contributing to an additional 10kg weight saving throughout the cabin.

Both the updated ceiling and sidewall offer a more seamless and smoother overall appearance compared with the previous design and could also become available for retrofit on in-service A330 Family aircraft.

The new door-frame lining is being introduced in parallel. Its design simplifies installation and replacement by reducing the number of parts, while contributing to an additional 5 kg of weight savings. The new lining also enhances the aesthetic appearance around the door thanks to its refined geometry.

The other option in the A330neo, which is currently offered in the A350, is Gentex's electro-dimmable windows (EDWs). These latest generation of EDWs are seamlessly adjustable, darken quickly and can effectively block more than 99.999% of visible light as well as the infra-red energy from the sun. Installation of the A330neos' new sidewall panel will allow easy clip-in replacement or interchangeability between the electro-mechanical shade and the EDW parts.

Airbus continually updates and enhances the A330neo Family in all areas. More recently, EASA has certified a new incremental package for the A330-900 (neo) which provides improved performance and versatility for operators, while delivering enhanced economics with extra revenue payload. This certification paves the way for first entry-into-service of the modification with Condor Flugdienst, the German leisure airline, on its A330neo fleet. Subsequently the package – known as 'Step-4' – will be available as a line fit option for new A330neo customer deliveries.

The package comprises three main features: (a) 'Enhanced Take Off Configurations' (ETOC) – which provides the pilot with additional flap positions; (b) faster landing gear retraction sequences with updated landing gear & doors actuators; and (c) 'Automatic Landing Gear Door Opening' (ALGDO) – which, if an engine failure is detected during the take-off run, automatically commands the landing gear doors to open one second after the aircraft becomes airborne.

These functions focus on enhancing the aircraft's low-speed performance. This is achieved by further maximising lift and reducing drag during the take-off and initial climb segments.

Step-4 enables operators to benefit from a significant extra take-off-weight uplift capability – translating into up to six metric tonnes more revenue-generating payload and/

or range-increasing fuel in some airports, and around 2.6 metric tonnes on average over the airports most flown by widebody aircraft. At other, even more runway-restricted airports, the net gain could be as much as seven tonnes – without increasing the engines' thrust.

Qantas enhances cabin

Qantas is upgrading the Economy cabins of ten A330-200 aircraft, as part of a multimillion dollar refurbishment programme. The aircraft are used on routes between Australia and Hong Kong, Singapore and Tokyo.

The next generation cabin upgrades include installing brand-new economy seats that have been designed with extra customer comfort for Qantas' Project Sunrise ultra-long haul flights, 4K OLED 13.3in entertainment

ABOVE • *Hi-Fly's first A330neo. The aircraft is configured with 371 seats in a two-class layout, with 18 high-comfort lie-flat, business-class seats and 353 economy seats.* AIRBUS - MASTER FILMS - GUILLAUME FRAYSSE

BELOW • *Japan Airlines' (JAL) first A350 XWB at Airbus headquarters in Toulouse, France. The A350-900 is the first aircraft produced by Airbus for JAL.* AIRBUS

touchscreens with the latest generation user interface (20% larger than the existing screen), and USB-C fast charging and Bluetooth audio connectivity. Other key elements of the A330 cabin upgrade programme include new mood lighting and the replacement of all curtains and carpets.

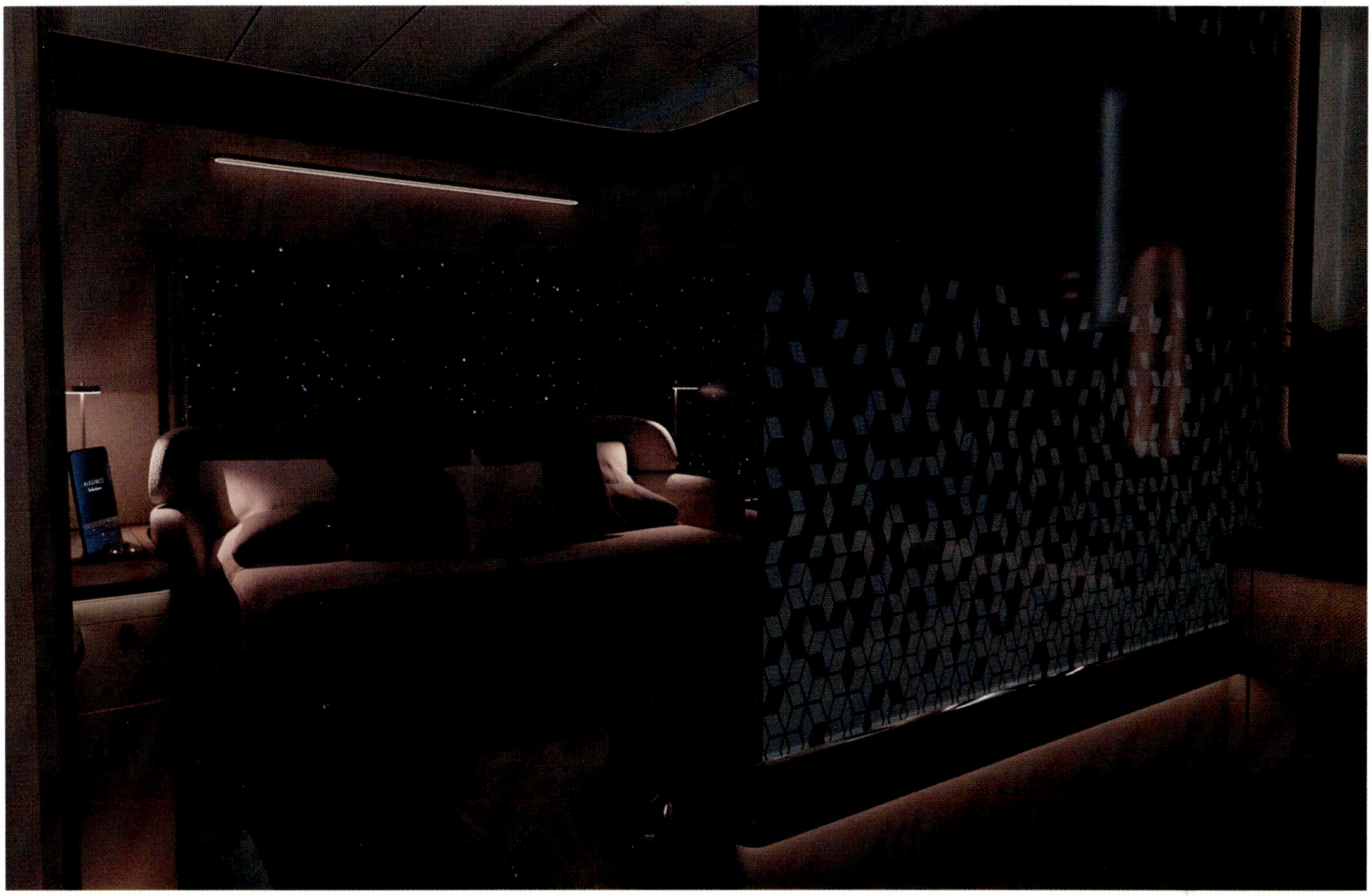

The existing business suites with fully-flat beds will remain on the aircraft. They continue to receive positive feedback from customers and are the same product that feature on Qantas' A380 and 787 Dreamliner fleet.

Work on the first A330 is expected to start in mid-2025 in Qantas' Brisbane maintenance facility with

the first refurbished aircraft entering service by the end of the calendar year. The refurbishment programme is expected to be completed by the end of 2026.

Qantas has also started its international Wi-Fi roll out across the A330 fleet. Fast and free Wi-Fi is expected to be available for Qantas flights on some routes in Asia using the Wi-Fi enabled A330 aircraft from December 2025.

The final piece of the airline's jet fleet renewal programme is a firm order for 24 aircraft to progressively replace its existing A330s – 12 Airbus A350s and 12 Boeing 787s arriving from FY27 into the next decade.

The longer range delivered by the 787 and A350 aircraft on order means they will be able to operate all the routes the A330s currently operate, as well as open up new ones. The A330 aircraft being upgraded are scheduled to leave the Qantas fleet towards the end of the replacement programme.

While some airlines are modernising their fleets with the A330neo, others have turned to the A350.

New First-Class

With increasing demand for first-class cabins on the Airbus flagship, the A350-1000, the airframer has revealed its latest concept for the most premium of cabins in the skies.

Conceived by its in-house design team, the Master Suite, which is located in the centre between the two aisles, accommodates two passengers, offering them exclusive access to a dedicated lavatory, changing area, bar and a double bed.

To accommodate the new '1-1-1' layout (i.e. three suites abreast) in the A350-1000, the floor area between Doors-1 to Doors-2 on the A350-1000 is fully maximised to dedicate as much space as possible for the new first-class section. In particular, floorspace which was previously taken up by lavatories or stowage, is now freed-up by relocating them outside of the main revenue (i.e. passenger accommodation) area in a new centre module just behind Doors-1, opposite the cockpit door. Additional privacy for passengers in the suites is provided by also relocating the access stairs to the Forward Crew Rest Compartment (FCRC) in the new centre module.

The large size and high ceilings of the A350-1000 make it the ideal choice for airlines to install their most premium product. Moreover, its unique interior proportions can be further complemented by new fascia and sculptured ceiling panels which provide an even greater sense of space, as well as an integrated welcome lighting panel at Doors-1 for extra ambience.

Finnair completes renewal programme

Ahead of its 100th birthday in 2023, Finnair unveiled a €200m investment, the result of four years development, to completely renew the cabins of its eight A330 and 19 A350 aircraft. The long-haul widebody fleet renewal was completed in 2024.

In business-class, the airline was the launch customer for the AirLounge seat, which draws inspiration from lounge furniture. Complicated seat mechanisms have been removed, instead replaced with unique 3D fixed shell lounge space, providing a larger flexible space, and enabling a wide variety of sitting and sleeping positions. Flexible infill panels on the seat base allow for a large, flat surface to create a bed, complete with mattress, duvet, and pillows from Finnish design house Marimekko, or extended lounge space. The high cocoon-like shell of the seat provides privacy, while the divider between central seats can be lowered when travelling with a companion.

The in-seat lighting complements new cabin mood lighting designed in partnership with Jetlite to combat the effects of jetlag. The design scheme is inspired by Nordic nature, complete with the northern lights as the cabin is dimmed for sleep. PriestmanGoode of London originally

BELOW • *The nose of an A330 in final assembly.* AIRBUS SAS 2022 HERVÉ GOUSSÉ - MASTER FILMS

conceived the seat which was further developed by Collins Aerospace, with customisation and final design execution by Finnair and its appointed design partner, Tangerine.

Other features include various storage options, a flexible table, internet connectivity, and in-seat charging including wireless mobile charging. The inflight entertainment system comes with a new more user-friendly, customised interface and a wider 18in screen.

The main entrance for all cabin classes has a stylish new entry area and a refreshment bar, creating a striking impression for customers and new service opportunities for cabin crew.

Finnair's new premium economy cabin was installed in all its long-haul aircraft for the first time. The new cabin class is situated in its own intimate and dedicated cabin with a maximum of just 26 passengers per aircraft, providing approximately 50% more space than economy-class.

Finnair is also the launch customer of the Haeco Vector premium seat which has been heavily adapted

*ABOVE • **The nose of a China Southern Airlines A350-900.*** AIRBUS – MASTER FILMS – HERVÉ GOUSSÉ

*RIGHT • **Air Caraïbes (a member airline of Groupe Dubreuil) was the first French operator of the A350-1000. It operates it on routes from Paris to the French Caribbean.*** AIRBUS SAS 2019 PASCAL PIGEYRE – MASTER FILMS

*BELOW • **Fiji Airways' first A350-900, delivered in November 2019, is configured in a two-class layout with 334 seats, and was the launch carrier from the South Pacific region.*** AIRBUS – MASTER FILMS – PHILIPPE MASLCET

ABOVE • *European leisure group TUI was the UK launch operator for the Boeing 787-8 in 2013 and has subsequently added the 787-9.* BOEING

and customised by Finnair and Tangerine. Key features include generous storage, a 13in IFE screen, and large and sturdy single-leaf meal tray table. Attention has been paid to comfort and ergonomics, with a waterfall leg rest, generous 8in recline, memory foam cushions and six-way adjustable headrest, which can be paired with a separate neck pillow.

The airline has also invested in a refresh of its long-haul economy-class, to provide customers with a more restful ambiance for their long-haul flight. New lighter seats for Finnair's A330 aircraft and three new A350 aircraft offer enhanced ergonomics, personal stowage options, USB A and C connectivity, and a larger inflight entertainment screen with an updated user interface.

Singapore Airlines reveals upgrades

Singapore Airlines (SIA) is investing S$1.1bn in a multi-year programme to install its all-new long-haul cabin products across 41 Airbus A350-900 long-haul and ultra-long-range (ULR) aircraft.

In a significant milestone, the airline will introduce a first-class cabin in its seven A350-900ULR aircraft. Business-class customers will enjoy SIA's upcoming business-class seats, featuring innovative designs that will offer even greater levels of privacy, comfort, and convenience in all 41 aircraft.

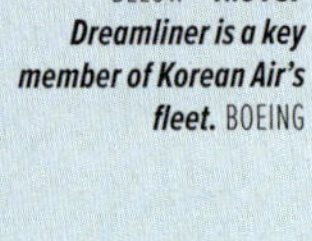

BELOW • *The 787 Dreamliner is a key member of Korean Air's fleet.* BOEING

These A350-900 first-class and business-class products are designed from the ground up, and are the same seat designs

that will feature on SIA's upcoming Boeing 777-9 aircraft. premium economy-class and economy-class cabins will also be refreshed.

Complementing the cabin products, the next version of SIA's KrisWorld in-flight entertainment (IFE) system will offer greater personalisation and an extensive range of lifestyle options across all cabin classes. First-class and business-class seats will also feature new in-flight entertainment screens.

SIA Engineering will retrofit the aircraft in Singapore. The first retrofitted A350-900 long-haul aircraft is expected to enter service in the second quarter of 2026, while the first A350-900ULR variant will follow in the first quarter of 2027. The entire programme is targeted for completion by the end of 2030.

Post-retrofit, the 34 A350-900 long-haul aircraft will be configured with 42 business-class seats, 24 premium economy-class seats, and 192 economy-class seats. The seven A350-900ULR variants will feature four first-class seats, 70 business-class seats, and 58 premium economy-class seats.

Retrofit revelry

Airbus will oversee the retrofitting of Thai Airways International (THAI) A350s, with upgrades including modernised and elevated 'Royal Silk' business-class seats, new premium economy-class seats and economy-class

ABOVE • *In 2012, Polish carrier LOT became the first European airline to take delivery of the 787.* BOEING

seats, as well as an improved in-flight entertainment system that offers a seamless travel experience across THAI's network

The cabin modernisation is expected to start from 2028. The retrofitted aircraft are expected to re-enter service in phases, ensuring minimal impact to THAI's flight operations.

Elsewhere, China Southern Airlines has appointed international design agency, Tangerine, to visualise the interiors for its next-generation wide-body and narrow-body flagship aircraft.

As part of its ongoing fleet modernisation, China Southern Airlines is introducing the new A350-900 and A321NX

aircraft – two dual flagship models designed to elevate the passenger experience to unprecedented levels.

Tangerine is designing the interiors of 10 A350-900 aircraft and the 20 new generation A321NX. The new A350-900 cabins will feature four private cabins, 24 independent business-class seats and 307 economy-class seats.

According to Weiwei He, Director at Tangerine: "The new interior design will evoke a distinctly oriental theme, highlighting China Southern's core brand values of 'affinity' and 'refinement.' Our goal is to create a cabin interior that resonates with passengers worldwide while proudly celebrating China Southern Airlines' rich cultural heritage."

RIGHT • *In 2016 Hainan Airlines became China's first operator of both the 787-8 and 787-9 variants of the Dreamliner family.* BOEING

BELOW • *Flag carrier Air Greenland selected Airbus' A330-800 to secure operations linking the Arctic island with neighbouring Denmark.* AIRBUS

Cargo
All packages large and small

The versatility and capacity offered by widebodies make them an ideal choice for freight services. Whether it's production models or conversions, the big two, Boeing and Airbus, have the aircraft and solutions, to ensure the smooth flow of international commerce.

ABOVE • *During 2021, Air Canada introduced its first converted Boeing 767-300ER Freighter which made its inaugural commercial flight from Toronto to Vancouver to support the Canadian supply chain. These new freighters are marking the start of a new chapter for Air Canada Cargo.* AIR CANADA CARGO

RIGHT • *Delta was one of the first US airlines granted permission to use the overhead bins on its widebody aircraft to carry mail, allowing it to increase capacity on cargo-only charters.* DELTA

According to global aviation data firm Cirium, the COVID-19 pandemic and its consequences had a devasting effect on the aviation industry, wiping out 21 years of global passenger traffic growth in a matter of months. In the US alone, air travel dropped 95% compared to 2019, while globally, passenger traffic was estimated to be down 67% compared to 2019.

At the height of the pandemic, Cirium data showed 63% of global passenger aircraft (16,000 aircraft) were grounded or 'in storage' as airlines drastically cut flights due to widespread travel restrictions. Among this desolation, cargo offered a bright spot for airlines. For many operators, 2020 saw air cargo become a vital source of revenues, despite weakened demand, but one facing a challenge – a reduction in belly capacity caused by the grounding of passenger fleets. Salvation came from reusing passenger cabins to carry cargo, in particular medical supplies, and airline regulators were quick to grant temporary consent for the purpose.

The rise of the 'preighter'

Delta can trace its cargo operations back to August 1946, when it launched scheduled domestic services, before expanding internationally in 1953. That initial flight saw Delta carry 200lb of freshly picked mushrooms loaded aboard a DC-3 destined for Atlanta. That first week of operation in 1946 the airline carried a 64-year-old person; a $1,500 soup tureen; 1,100lb of auto parts boxed in six crates; 450lb of candy and a box of silver coins.

In March 2020, in response to its corporate customers informing the airline they needed help transporting cargo during this time of uncertainty and change, Delta Cargo launched charter operations. Thirteen US airports participated in this programme, as well as over 70 available international destination airports.

Following approval from the US Federal Aviation Administration (FAA), the airline increased its cargo capacity by utilising the overhead bin space of its widebody aircraft, allowing capacity to be maximised on cargo-only charters. The first flights to carry cargo this way saw mail shipped both to and from Chicago and Frankfurt, Germany in April.

Across the whole of 2020, it was estimated that as many as 200 airlines operated more than 2,500 of these so-called 'preighter' flights – the term a marriage of 'passenger' and 'freighter' attributed to Lufthansa boss Carsten Spohr. But some airlines went a step further. Air Canada entered cargo-only flights in March 2020. In addition to transporting freight on their aircraft operating scheduled passenger services, Air Canada Cargo also transports freight on cargo-only flights using Air Canada's mainline widebody Boeing 777s, Boeing 787s and Boeing 777s. With certification and approval by Transport Canada, the airline became the first in the world to remove seats for cargo in the cabin, when it reconfigured the cabins of

ABOVE • Emirates' 'mini-freighter' saw ten Boeing 777-300ER aircraft modified to carry cargo, removing economy-class seating to create space for an additional 17 tonnes of cargo in the cabin. EMIRATES

BELOW • In just six days, Avianor designed, developed, and implemented a technical solution to remove a total of 1,266 passenger seats from three Air Canada 777-300ER aircraft, and designed loading areas for light boxes under cargo nets. AIR CANADA

ABOVE • *Emirates SkyWheels. In 2016, Emirates SkyCargo transported a collection of rare classic Ferrari cars to Dubai for the inaugural Gulf Concours event.* EMIRATES

four Boeing 777-300ERs, the largest aircraft in its fleet, and three Airbus A330s. Three Boeing 777-300ER aircraft were converted by Avianor, an aircraft maintenance and cabin integration specialist, at its Montreal-Mirabel, Canada facility. The company developed a specific engineering solution to remove 422 passenger seats and designate cargo loading zones for light weight boxes containing medical equipment and restrained with cargo nets. The reconfigured cabins doubled the aircraft's cargo carrying capacity to 89.63 tons of cargo, equivalent to nearly 9m medical masks.

Each of Air Canada's reconfigured A330s were able to carry an additional 16,750kg of cargo. The first A330 cargo-in-cabin flight arrived in Montreal from Tel Aviv, Israel with a mix of mail, e-commerce packages, and face masks loaded in the cabin. There was also a variety of goods in

RIGHT • *Finnair is the launch customer for Airbus and Lufthansa Technik's Temporary Cargo Cabin solution for A330 aircraft, which increases cargo transportation capacity in the cabin for short-term use.* AIRBUS

the belly, including perishable foods and freshly cut Mother's Day flowers. In the space of a few months, early July 2021 to be precise, Air Canada Cargo reached its 10,000th cargo-only flight. The on-demand flight was operated by a Boeing 789. In December 2021, Air Canada took delivery of the first of eight dedicated freighters providing additional capacity to key destinations in Europe and the Americas. This aircraft was initially intended to support the shipping community during the busy peak season.

Converting Boeing 767-300ER passenger aircraft to freighters allows Air Canada Cargo to offer five different main deck configurations, increasing the overall capacity of each aircraft to over 57 tonnes (or 438m^3), with approximately 75% of this capacity on the main deck.

Looking at the wider picture, between March and December 2020, it was estimated that 155 aircraft had all or most of their passenger seats removed in order to transport more cargo in their cabins.

ABOVE • Singapore Airlines is renewing its freighter fleet and will become the first operator of the Airbus A350F in 2025. AIRBUS

BELOW • The 777 Freighter is the best-selling freighter ever, with DHL an enthusiastic operator. DHL

According to Cirium, widebodies made up most cabin cargo fleets. Airbus and Boeing twin-aisle jets accounted for 80% of the aircraft, including 49 A330s and 45 Boeing 777s operated by 16 different airlines, such as Lufthansa (10 A330s), China Eastern Airlines (14 A330s) and Emirates.

The mini-freighter

With an average age of under six years, the widebodied fleet of aircraft used by Emirates SkyCargo, the freight division of the Middle Eastern airline, are amongst the youngest in the world. Its dedicated freighter fleet includes Airbus A380-800s, Boeing 777-300s and Boeing 777Fs. To supplement capacity during the pandemic, Emirates SkyCargo operated a fleet of 14 Boeing 777-300ERs with seats removed from the economy class cabin.

Each aircraft required nearly 640 man-hours of work for the modification which saw engineers remove 305 economy seats per aircraft, fixing safety equipment

ABOVE • *KLM's Cargo-in-Cabin significantly increases capacity equating to around six large pallets in the belly or 40% of the total cargo capacity on a 777-300.* KLM

BELOW • *UPS was the first customer of the 767 Freighter, and recently ordered 19 more.* UPS

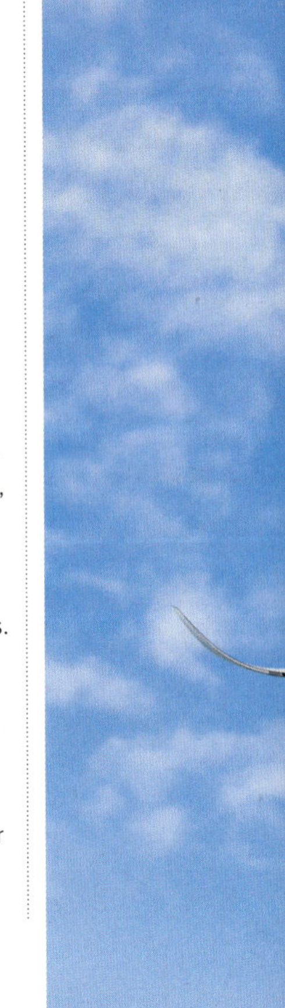

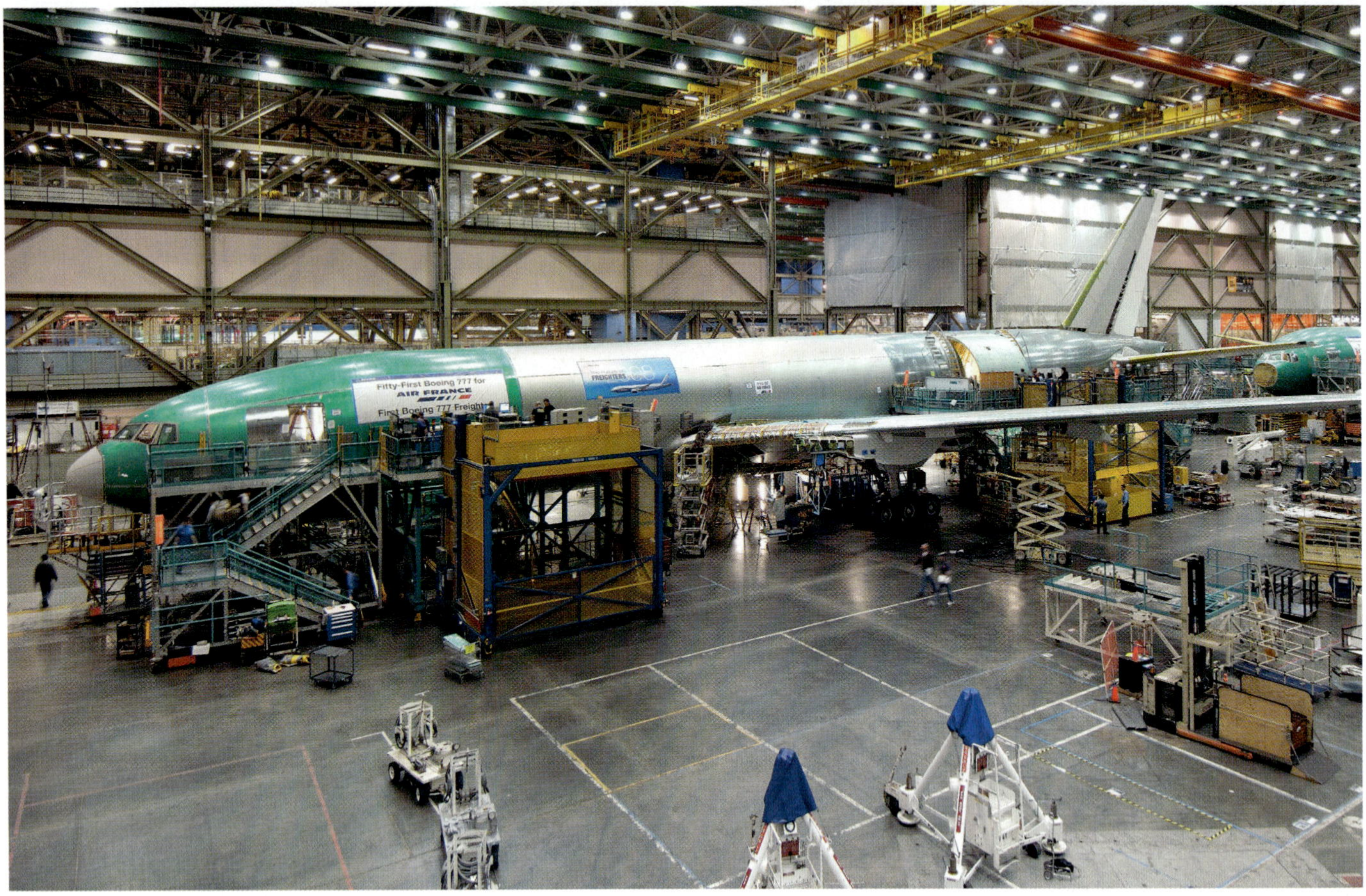

ABOVE • ***The first Boeing 777 Freighter enters final assembly before delivery to launch customer Air France.*** BOEING

and implementing regular load bearing tests during the process. The result created space for up to 17 tonnes or 132m^3 of additional cargo capacity per flight on top of the 40-50 tonne cargo capacity in the belly hold of the widebody passenger aircraft. Emirates had previously responded to customer demands for increased cargo operations with measures such as flying passenger aircraft only with bell hold cargo and loading cargo in the overhead cabin bins and on passenger seats.

Emirates SkyCargo also utilised its Airbus A380 aircraft to transport around 50 tonnes of cargo per flight in the belly of the aircraft on select cargo charter operations. The first dedicated Emirates A380 'mini-freighter' transported medical supplies between Seoul, South Korea, and Amsterdam, Netherlands via Dubai.

A reversible solution

A year later, and many of these temporary exemptions were expiring. In response, Airbus and Lufthansa Technik introduced the 'Temporary Cargo Cabin', a reversible cargo-in-cabin solution for the A330 that enables the modification of a passenger cabin into a cargo hold and back, by removing seats, monuments, cabling and temporarily blocking water supply interfaces. Finnair became the first airline to take advantage of the solution, modifying one of its Airbus A330-300s to carry commercial, non-dangerous goods in the main passenger deck.

Under the solution, standard TSO (Technical Standard Order) approved pallets with special brackets are installed on the seat tracks in the centre column of the aircraft with additional positions created in adjacent areas to an optimal use of the A330 cabin. The bulk cargo is secured with standard TSO approved nets. As a result, cargo capacity is increased by up to 15 tonnes of additional payload depending on aircraft configuration and customer needs. Boosted by e-commerce and delays in transporting goods by sea, it is expected that express freight will grow by 4.7% per year and general cargo by 2.7%.

Medium widebody freighters have capacities of 40 to 80 tonnes, and are supplied through both conversion and production, with the product mix influenced by operator requirements as well as feedstock availability. Freighter models include the Boeing 767, Boeing DC-10, Airbus A300/A310 and Airbus A330. Airbus sees a need over the next 20 years for approximately 2,440 freighters, of which 880 will be new-build, with about half of the total demand required in the mid-sized segment of the A330 – including some 900 conversions.

The cost to convert

Analysts believe that as a rule of thumb the target price for a 20-year-old converted freighter is 25% - 30% of the price of a new freighter. For example, a new production medium widebody aircraft is over $70m, while a new production large widebody aircraft will set you back over $150m.

Compare this to the cost of conversions. According to Jon Whaley, senior aviation analyst at IBA, the cost of converting older generation aircraft ranges from $2.5m for the Boeing 737-300, $2.8m for the 737-400, $5m for a 757-200 and $13 to 15m for the 767-300ER. For new generation aircraft airlines could find themselves paying $3.5m for converting a 737-700, $4m for a 737-800, and $15m to $16m for an A330-200/300.

The popularity of the passenger A330 aircraft and their large numbers in service provides a rich source (feedstock) of aircraft to support the freighter conversion for many years. More than 1,600 A330s have been ordered, with over 1,300 delivered to date since the type's service entry in 1994. The Airbus A330P2F programme offers a passenger-to-freighter conversion opportunity for A330s that have been retired from passenger service.

Both the A330-200 and A330-300 versions are eligible for the P2F conversion, with the longer-fuselage A330-300P2F ideally suited for express carriers, and the A330-200P2F

optimised for higher-density freight and longer-range performance.

In December 2017, DHL Express became the first operator to take delivery of an A330-300P2F converted aircraft from Elbe Flugzeugwerke (EFW), the joint venture between ST Aerospace and Airbus. The German logistics company is operating its A330-300P2F fleet in Europe and Asia as well as on transatlantic flights from Leipzig, Germany to the US. DHL Express has 18 A330-300P2F on order in total.

BELOW • *Airbus has firmed up an order for the purchase of four A350F freighter aircraft from CMA CGM AIR CARGO, the recently launched air cargo activity of CMA CGM Group.* AIRBUS

Mid-size sibling

In 2010, Airbus introduced the mid-size freighter, the A330-200F, based on the A330-200 passenger jetliner, and produced on the same Toulouse, France final assembly line as other A330 and A340 Family aircraft. According to Airbus, the A300-200F offers 35% lower operating costs per tonne compared to larger freighters, as well as optimised load factors. Additionally, through optimising the fuselage cross-section, and being able to offer different pallet

A330P2F, A330-200F and A350F characteristics

	A330P2F	A330-200F	A350F
Overall length	63.66m (208ft 10in)	58.82m (193ft)	70.80m (232ft 3in)
Cabin length	50.4m (165ft 4in)	45.00m (147ft 8in)	52m (170ft 8in)
Fuselage width	5.64m (18ft 5in)	5.64m (18ft 5in)	5.96m (19ft 5in)
Max cabin width	5.26m (17ft 3in)	5.26m (17ft 3in)	5.4m (17ft 9in)
Wingspan	60.30m (197ft 8in)	60.30m (197ft 8in)	64.75m (212ft 4in)
Height	16.79m (55ft 1in)	17.39m (57ft 1in)	17.80m (58ft 2in)
Max payload	62 tonnes (136,687lb)	61 tonnes (134,482lb)	109 tonnes (240,304lb)
Pallets or containers main deck	Up to 27 pallets	Up to 23 pallets	30 pallets or 30x AM-base containers
underfloor	11 pallets or 32 LD3 (8 pallets + 2 LD3 containers)	8 pallets + 2 LD3 containers or 26 LD3 (8 pallets + 2 LD3 containers)	12 pallets or 40xLD3 containers*
Range	6,780km (3,660nm)	7,400km (4,150nm)	8,700km (4,700nm)
Mmo	0.86	0.86	N/A
Max ramp weight	233.9 tonnes (515,661lb)	233.9 tonnes (515,661lb)	N/A
Max take-off weight	233 tonnes (513,677lb)	233 tonnes (513,677lb)	319 tonnes (703,275lb)
Max landing weight	182 tonnes (401,241lb)	187.0 tonnes (412,264lb)	250 tonnes (551,156lb)

*Pallet or container General cargo layout - Lower deck
Source: Airbus

and container sizes through its large main deck cargo door (an electrically controlled and hydraulically operated aperture of 141 x 101in) the aircraft offers 30% more volume than any freighter in its class. Airbus also says the A330-200F flies 20% further and has a cost per tonne that is 13% lower than its direct competitor.

With a capability of carrying 65-to-70 tonnes of payload, with a range that stretches from 3,200nm up to 4,000nm, the A330-200F can transport up to 23 side-by-side pallets on its main deck, with flexibility for additional arrangements such as single-row loading of 16 pallets, and a mix of nine AMA containers with four pallets. The lower-deck cargo hold accepts up to 26 LD3 containers, plus 19.7m³ of bulk cargo.

At the 2010 Farnborough Airshow, Etihad Airways became the first customer to receive an A330-200F, however in 2018, the airline began the process of disposing of its five A330-200Fs, having withdrawn them from service and placed them in storage in Abu Dhabi International Airport and Spain's Teruel Airport. Hong Kong Airlines and Turkish Airlines were other first movers for the freighter.

A new addition

In early 2021, Airbus received board of directors' approval for a freighter derivative of the A350 designed to meet the imminent wave of large freighter replacements and the evolving environmental requirements, shaping the future of airfreight. The A350F will be powered by the latest technology, fuel-efficient Rolls-Royce Trent-XWB97 engines.

As a direct replacement for Boeing's 777F, the A350F will feature a large main deck cargo door and a fuselage length optimised for cargo operations offering a 109 tonnes payload capability (+3t payload/11% more volume and an additional five pallet positions than its 777F competitor).

According to Airbus, such economics will result in up to $21m extra revenue for the operating airline, as well as lower

BELOW • An unpainted A330-200F takes off ahead of delivery to Qatar Airways. AIRBUS - MASTER FILMS - HERVÉ GOUSSÉ

ABOVE • *During the pandemic, Ethiopian used its entire A350-900 fleet for cargo operations, with seven out of its 16 extra-wide body aircraft having been converted to freighters by removing all economy seats.* AIRBUS SAS 2020 PHILIPPE MASCLET - MASTER FILMS

BELOW • *Part of Lufthansa Cargo's fleet since August 2020, Lufthansa Cargo Boeing 777F with the registration D-ALFH, has officially been* Namaste India. LUFTHANSA CARGO, OLIVER RÖSER

maintenance costs of $16m in comparison to the 777F. To date, five airlines have signed up to order nearly 30 aircraft.

Singapore Airlines (SIA) will become the launch customer for the A350F when it takes its first delivery in the fourth quarter of 2025. The airline has ordered seven aircraft with options for five more which will gradually replace its seven Boeing 747-400Fs.

"This order underscores the importance of the cargo market to the SIA Group. The introduction of the A350F will enhance our capabilities in this key sector, ensuring that we are ready for the growth opportunities that will arise in the coming years," commented Goh Choon Phong, chief executive officer, Singapore Airlines, at the signing of the order during the 2022 Singapore Air Show.

The enthusiasm was shared by Chin Yau Seng, senior vice president cargo, Singapore Airlines, who added that

the new aircraft will "bolster our efforts to tap demand from key verticals as it is designed to carry various types of special cargo, ranging from outsized equipment such as aircraft engines to temperature-sensitive shipments." The latter includes temperature-controlled pharmaceutical cargo and of perishables such as chilled meat, fresh fruit, and flowers.

The air show also saw Etihad Airways sign a Letter of Intent (LoI) for seven A350F freighters, while Air France-KLM ordered four of them. Shipping and logistics company, CMA CGM Group has also committed to the purchase of four A350F freighter aircraft, to be operated by CMA CGM AIR CARGO, the air cargo activity of the Group. More recently, Cathay Cargo, the cargo division of Cathay Group signed a purchase agreement for six aircraft, whilst at the time of writing, STARLUX Cargo has become the latest customer, with an order for 10 A350F freighters.

Boeing dominates

Boeing is equally bullish about the future demand for cargo. In its latest biennial World Air Cargo Forecast (WACF), the freighter fleet forecast calls for 3,900 airplanes in service by 2043, a two-thirds increase from the in-service 2023 fleet of 2,340. Of this, 785 aircraft will be large widebodies and 785 medium widebodies.

Boeing has an extensive freighter family. This includes the 747-8F, the only commercial freighter with nose loading capability, and the pioneer of widebody freighters. In March 1972, Lufthansa received the first 747-200.

"The ability to ship more goods by air changed global trade overnight," says Darren Hulst, Boeing's vice president of commercial marketing. "People around the world could receive goods in days instead of months. Boeing freighters played a significant role in that, and they continue to define the art of the possible today."

Fifty years later and 90% of the world's freighter capacity belongs to Boeing freighters, whose family includes the 777F; 767-300F; 767-300BCF (Boeing Conversion Freighter) and the 737-800BCF.

Boeing bets on the 777-8

To safeguard its dominance, Boeing has also introduced its latest model, the 777-8F, the newest member of the 777X family, set for deliveries in 2028. With a range of 4,410nm (8,167km), the 777-8 Freighter has a maximum structural payload of 118 tonnes, close to that of the 747-400F, allowing customers to make fewer stops and reduce landing fees on long-haul routes.

Qatar Airways will be the 777-8 Freighter launch customer with a firm order for 34 jets and options for 16 more, a total purchase that would be worth more than $20bn at current list prices and the largest freighter commitment in Boeing history by value.

"We certainly push Boeing hard to deliver upon our expectations, and the team at Boeing consistently strives to meet and exceed our expectations, giving the opportunity for us to be here today to launch the most significant new freighter aircraft for a generation," commented Akbar Al Baker the then Qatar Airways group chief executive.

Longstanding customer Ethiopian Airlines is set to become the second purchaser, having signed a memorandum of understanding (MOU) with the intent to acquire five 777-8 Freighters. "In our vision 2035, we are planning to expand our cargo and logistics business to be one of the largest global multimodal logistics providers in all continents. To this effect we are increasing our dedicated freighter fleet with the latest technology, fuel efficient and environment-friendly airplanes of the 21st century," stated their group CEO Tewolde Gebremariam. "The new 777-8 Freighters will be instrumental in this long journey of growth agenda."

A popular choice

The 777 Freighter is Boeing's best-selling freighter of all time. It has a range of 4,970nm (9,200km), and can carry a maximum structural payload of 107 tonnes (235,900lb). More than 300 of the type have been ordered since the programme began in 2005.

DHL Express reinforced its partnership with Boeing under an ongoing modernisation of its airfreight fleet investing in eight new 777Fs, for entry on trans-Pacific and intercontinental routes between Asia and Europe. Between 2018 and 2022, DHL bought 28 new B777-200F freighters from Boeing - 18 of those aircraft are currently in service. The remaining aircraft will be delivered by the end of 2025. The aircraft forms the backbone of DHL's intercontinental air network.

DHL Express has ordered nine Mammoth-converted B777-200LR freighters from Jetran. The first cargo aircraft were delivered in 2024, with the remaining aircraft to be supplied until early 2027. The Mammoth converted B777-200LR freighter promises similar characteristics and benefits as the production freighter and is an ideal fit for DHL. With a payload capacity of 102 tons and a range of 9,200km, the B777F has the largest capacity and range of all twin-engine freighter aircraft and is more reliable than older B747 planes. It is also more fuel-efficient and reduces CO_2 emissions by 18% compared to legacy airplanes.

Other significant orders have come from the likes of National Airlines, who in 2024 ordered four 777Fs with deliveries scheduled to begin in the next several years, Emirates SkyCargo (10 aircraft), and Turkish Airlines (4 aircraft), who, with its most recent order, will operate 12 777F freighters.

According to Turkish Airlines Chief Cargo Officer Ali Türk, the addition of these Boeing 777 Freighters will not only enhance the airline's operational capabilities but also serve as another step in its strategic vision to reach the top of air cargo sector worldwide.

In 2024, Maersk Air Cargo took delivery of its two new Boeing 777Fs, ordered as part of the modernisation of its fleet. Both are deployed on Maersk's existing Europe-China route with up to six weekly flights. Narin Phol, Executive Vice President and Chief Product Officer (CPO) for Logistics and Services at Maersk, said of the deliveries, "From a commercial perspective the two Boeing 777Fs are a giant leap in terms of what we can offer our air freight customers going forward. Besides enabling a much more efficient route structuring our 777Fs will improve the availability of space for our customers as we see a growing demand for integrated supply chain solutions which include air."

Maersk is also the only company in the UK licenced to operate a Boeing 767-200.

Economic merits

Boeing has more than 40 years of experience in passenger-to-freighter conversions. The 737-800BCF carries more payload – up to 23.9 tonnes (52,800lb) – and flies farther – 2,025nm (3,750km) compared to 737 classic freighters.

Dublin-headquartered ASL Aviation Holdings (ASL) has commitments and orders for 40 737-800BCFs. The aircraft will be converted by Boeing at approved MRO sites including STAECO in Jinan, China and at Boeing's London Gatwick MRO facility in the UK. "Boeing Converted

BELOW • *Between October 2020 and December 2021 Qantas became the first operator of the A321P2F when it took delivery of three aircraft, operated on domestic services on behalf of Australia Post.*
AIRBUS

Boeing 747-8F, 767F and 777-8 characteristics

	747-8F	Boeing 767F	777-8
Overall length	76.25m (250ft 2in)	54.9m (180ft 1in)	70.9m (232ft 6in)
Max cabin width	5.9m (19ft 3in)	4.7m (15ft 4in)	61m (20ft 1in)
Wingspan	68.45m (224ft 6in)	47.6m (156ft 2in)	71.8m (235ft 5in)
Height	19.4m (63ft 6in)	15.9m (52ft 2in)	19.5m (64ft)
Max payload	133.1 tonnes (295,000lb)	52.7 tonnes	112.3 tonnes
Pallets or containers main deck	34 pallets	24 contoured pallets	31 pallets
underfloor	12 pallets + 2 LD-1 containers	7 pallets + 2 LD-2 containers + bulk	13 pallets
Range	8,009km (4325nm)	11,158km (6025nm)	8,167km (4,410nm)
Mmo	0.90	0.80	0.92
Max ramp weight	449 tonnes (990,000lb)	185 tonnes (408,000lb)	N/A
Max take-off weight	449 tonnes (990,000lb)	185 tonnes (408,000lb)	448 tonnes (987,000lb)
Max landing weight	343 tonnes (756,186lb)	145 tonnes (319,670lb)	343.3 tonnes (756,186lb)

Source: Boeing

Freighters support progress towards sustainability goals by providing operators like those under the ASL Group umbrella an economical way to replace less efficient, older-generation freighters," said Jens Steinhagen, director of Boeing Converted Freighters.

During the pandemic, online sales accelerated putting pressure on cargo network capacity. In a perfect storm, shipment weights increased at a time when cargo capacity on passenger airlines bottomed out. To address the increased demand and protect service to destinations to which commercial flight services were reduced or suspended, airlines adapted their air network operations by adding more of their own dedicated flights with dedicated freighters. Going forward, cargo operators will continue to expand and modernise their network and intercontinental fleets.

RIGHT • *A Cargolux's 747-400ERF freighters, sporting a brand-new retro livery to celebrate the airline's 50 years of existence.* CARGOLUX

BELOW • *EVA Air uses its five Boeing 777 Freighters to bolster its fleet on transpacific and Asian routes.* BOEING

Jet Set Life

You don't have to be a head of state, billionaire, or corporation to experience the luxury of a widebody private jet. Regardless of the depth of your pockets, access to the comfort and convenience of private jets is now available to more of us.

Many of us will have flown on a widebody aircraft for long-haul, international travel, but only a lucky few will have experienced the private luxury of a VIP jet.

When Boeing launched Boeing Business Jet (BBJ) in 1996, Airbus was prompted to follow suit just a year later, launching Airbus Corporate Jets (ACJ) thereby initiating a new battleground between these old adversaries.

Launched as a joint venture between Boeing and General Electric, the BBJ targeted individuals, corporations, governments, armed forces, and heads of state, using a derivative of the commercial narrowbody 737-700 as its first platform, marrying the fuselage of the 737-700 and the strengthened wings and landing gear of the larger 737-800.

GE took delivery of the first business jet in the autumn of 1998, and it generated orders from several customers including golfer Greg Norman.

Further iterations followed with the introduction of the BBJ 2 in 1999 built on a 737-800 fuselage, and in 2006, it marked the occasion of its 10th anniversary with the launch of a new family member - the BBJ 3 based on the new Next-Generation 737-900ER (Extended Range).

Very Important Planes

Since 2006, the 787 and 747-8 have also been available for BBJ conversion, attracting business leaders and heads of state customers.

During the 2014 European Business Aviation Conference & Exhibition (EBACE) in Geneva, Boeing announced that widebody airplane orders accounted for more than one-third of Boeing's total VIP orders, outperforming the competition in this segment.

One of the first customers for the 787 BBJ was the now defunct PrivatAir, who became the first commercial business aviation specialist to offer the 787 to its customers. The order from the Geneva-based company was worth US$153m at 2006 list prices.

While the first BBJ 747-8 entered into service and was operated by an undisclosed customer, Hong Kong real estate tycoon Joseph Lau chose to go public with his purchase.

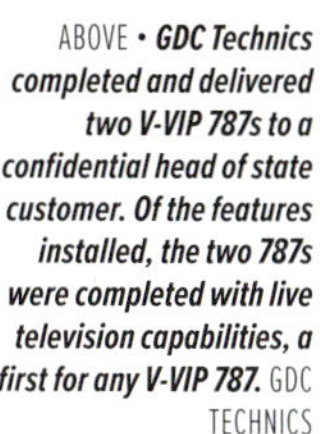

ABOVE • GDC Technics completed and delivered two V-VIP 787s to a confidential head of state customer. Of the features installed, the two 787s were completed with live television capabilities, a first for any V-VIP 787. GDC TECHNICS

RIGHT • The lounge onboard a BBJ 777X as conceived by Greenpoint Technologies, one of three design firms who visualised different interiors to showcase the cabin's adaptability. GREENPOINT TECHNOLOGIES

courtesy of Jet Aviation

courtesy of Unique Aircraft and ACA SD

ABOVE • *Jet Aviation was one of three design firms invited by Boeing to present interior concepts for the BBJ 777X.* JET AVIATION

LEFT • *The BBJ 3 was showcased for the first time in 2013*: BOEING

"The 787 VIP is an extremely attractive jet for wealthy and successful entrepreneurs, especially in Asia where business is conducted over long distances. The 787 has it all - long-range capability, advanced technology, and a spacious, comfortable cabin - attributes that are needed to conduct business around the world," said Boeing Business Jets president Steven Hill on the disclosure. "We are honoured by Mr Lau's confidence in Boeing jets and his relationship with Boeing Business Jets."

The VIP-configured 787-8 offers 2,404sq ft (223.3m^2) of cabin space. To enhance the passenger experience, windows on the 787 are 78% larger than those on the A330 and are placed higher on the fuselage for easier viewing. Catering to the personal preferences of the passenger, the windows can be electronically dimmed either at source or via panels located throughout the cabin.

Reflecting a desire for wellness inflight, the BBJ 787 pressurises its cabin 2,000 ft lower than competitor aircraft.

Other customers include the government of Poland, which operates the jet as a head of state aircraft. "We have a great airplane, which will be very well equipped. This airplane can run the country from the air," said Poland's Deputy Defense Minister Bartosz Kownacki commenting on the order. More recently, an unnamed VIP customer acquired two BBJ 787-9 aircraft, valued at $5,654m (2019 list prices).

Completion centres

Washington-based, Greenpoint Technologies has set out to become the world's leading Boeing 787 completion centre. To date, Greenpoint has been awarded seven V-VIP Boeing 787 interior completions, completing five.

RIGHT • *Crystal Skye, an 88-seat BBJ 777-200LR, was part of Crystal Luxury Air, the aviation arm of Crystal Cruises, and offered all-inclusive luxury air travel with a wide range of itineraries.* CRYSTAL CRUISES

In 2021, Greenpoint delivered the world's first V-VIP Boeing 787-9 interior completion to an undisclosed client. The company managed the completion from conception through redelivery, including the design, engineering, and integration of the custom-built interior.

Collaborating with the client's representatives, the result is an interior that blends state-of-the-art systems and technology with precise interior design detail. The main cabin caters to the client's distinct needs with private VIP areas and an expansive, multi-functional living space featuring woven fabrics, wood veneers, and intricate metallic details complemented by soft, indirect lighting.

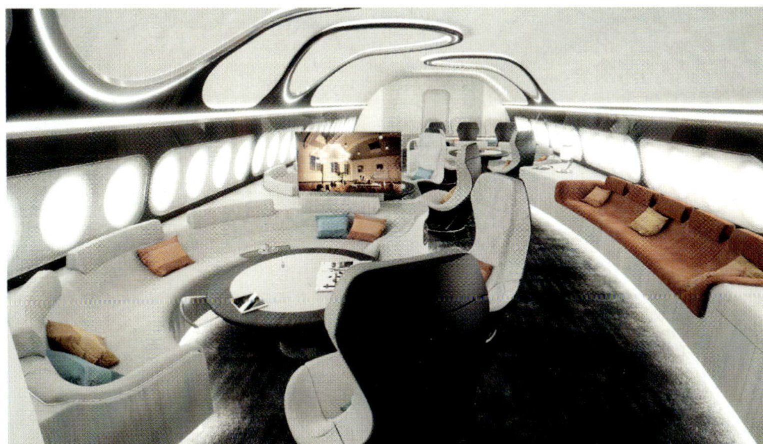

BELOW • *Harmony cabin concept - Lounge overview Harmony, from ACJ is suitable for the ACJ330neo family and ACJ350 XWB aircraft types.* AIRBUS CORPORATE JETS

BOTTOM • *With the ACJ330 as its platform, Explorer from Lufthansa Technik is a five-star hotel, which can fly almost anywhere.* LUFTHANSA TECHNIK/BRABUS

More recently, Greenpoint has been appointed by an undisclosed client for two V-VIP Boeing 787-9 interior completions. Partnered directly with the client to create interior designs tailored to their lifestyle and aircraft mission requirements, each interior will include private first-class suites and distinct V-VIP areas featuring elevated ceilings, a customised inflight entertainment system and communication technologies, and low cabin acoustic levels.

Dream Jet

Unveiled in Geneva, Switzerland at the 2016 EBACE, Kestrel Aviation Management managed the purchase, modification, and sale of the first-ever V-VIP custom Boeing Business Jet (BBJ) 787-8. This 40-seat corporate aircraft has nearly 9,800nm range and the ability to fly for 18.5 hours, 16,000km – the equivalent of London to Perth, Australia, non-stop.

The 787's cabin pressure is set to 6,000 feet at the height of 30,000 feet. The interior design was produced by Kestrel Aviation Management together with Pierrejean Design Studio of Paris, who took 2 1/2 years to style the cabin.

Features include a grand entry with high domed ceilings, hardwood flooring, sculpted doors, marble bathrooms, oversize shower, hand- tufted carpet with silk accents, and architectural pieces in unique materials. Tablets located throughout the cabin control lighting, video monitors, audio, window shades and flight attendant requests.

In August 2016, Deer Jet, a wholly owned subsidiary of HNA Group, took over the operation of the aircraft, which made its maiden flight months later. The price to charter the 787 Dream Jet was confirmed to be £55,000 per hour. Of the new addition to the Deer Jet fleet, Frank Fang, the company vice president said: "It showcases the signature service of Deer Jet which is inspired by the values of performance, elegance and distinction. Our goal is to provide the best flying experience for our customers and 'make travel an art'."

Extras

In 2014, the first BBJ 747-8 entered into service, operated by an undisclosed customer. That same year, Greenpoint Technologies patented the Aeroloft which provides 393sq ft (36.5m^2) of additional cabin space bringing the VIP-configured 747-8 to a total 5,179sq ft (481.2m^2) of cabin space.

Developed specifically for the BBJ 747-8, the Aeroloft is located above the main cabin between the upper deck and

ACJ330neo and ACJ350 technical characteristics

	ACJ330-800	ACJ330-900	ACJ350-900	ACJ350-1000
Length	58.82m (193ft)	63.66m (208ft 10in)	66.8m (219ft 2in)	73.79m (242ft 1in)
Height	17.39m (57ft 1in)	16.79m (55ft 1in)	17.05m (55ft 11in)	17.08m (56ft)
Fuselage width	5.64m (18ft 6in)	5.64m (18ft 6in)	5.96m (19ft 7in)	5.96m (19ft 7in)
Wingspan	64m (210ft)	64m (210ft)	64.75m (212ft 5in)	64.75m (212ft 5in)
Cabin length	45m (147ft 9in)	50.35m (165ft 2in)	51.04m (167ft 5in)	58.03m (190ft 5in)
Max cabin width	5.27m (17ft 3in)	5.27m (17ft 3in)	5.61m (18ft 5in)	5.61m (18ft 5in)
Cabin floor area	216m^2 (2,325sq ft)	243m^2 (2,616sq ft)	270m^2 (2,905sq ft)	308m^2 (3,315sq ft)
Max take-off weight	Up to 251 tonnes (553,400lb)	Up to 251 tonnes (553,400lb)	280 tonnes (606,200lb)	316 tonnes (696,200lb)
Max landing weight	186 tonnes (410,060lb)	191 tonnes (421,083lb)	205 tonnes (451,900lb)	236 tonnes (520,300lb)
Max zero fuel weight	176 tonnes (388,014lb)	181 tonnes (399,037lb)	192 tonnes (423,300lb)	223 tonnes (491,600lb)
Max fuel capacity	139,090 lit (36,750 US gal)	139,090 lit (136,750 US gal)	165,000 lit (43,588 US gal)	156,000 lit (41,210 US gal)
Engines	2x Rolls Royce Trent (2 x 72,000lbf)	2 x Rolls Royce Trent (2 x 72,000lbf)	2x Rolls Royce Trent XWB (2 x 84,000lbf)	2 x Rolls Royce Trent XWB (2 x 97,000lbf)
Typical cruise speed	M0.82	M0.82	M.085	M0.85
Max flight level	41,000ft	41,000ft	43,000ft	43,000ft

Source: Airbus

tail of the airplane. It boasts eight private sleeping berths and a changing room providing a comfortable rest area during flight.

Greenpoint has also patented Aerolift, a secure, self-contained method to transport individuals (up to four passengers or a wheelchair passenger with attendant) from the ground to the main deck on a Boeing VIP 747-8 aircraft.

The arrival of the BBJ 777

Towards the end of December 2018 Boeing Business launched the BBJ 777X, to 'redefine ultra-long range VIP travel'.

Customers can choose between two models: the BBJ 777-8 and BBJ 777-9. The BBJ 777-8 offers the longest range of 11,645nm (21,570km) and a spacious 3,256sq ft (302.5m^2) cabin.

The BBJ 777-9 provides an even larger cabin measuring 3,689sq ft (342.7m^2), while still offering ultra-long range of 11,000nm (20,370km).

To demonstrate the versatility of the airplane's spacious cabin, and almost unlimited interior design options, BBJ unveiled interior concepts from three leading design firms: Greenpoint Technologies, Jet Aviation, and Unique Aircraft Design. Each concept shows how the BBJ 777X can be transformed to suit the tastes of any VIP customer.

Luxury was also at the heart of Crystal Skye, an ex-Air Austral Boeing 777-200LR which was operated by Comlux Aruba on behalf of Crystal AirCruises, part of Crystal Cruises. Again, outfitted by Greenpoint Technologies, the BBJ B777-200LR was redesigned to accommodate 88 passengers. The interior installation began in August 2016 at Greenpoint's Moses Lake facility in Washington, focusing on exclusive features such as a 24-seat lounge with a central bar, sofas, custom coved ceilings, the largest wine cellar in the sky and ample space to socialise. Stone veneers, coloured LED lighting and other premium details adorn the extraordinary interior.

The Crystal Exclusive Class seat, a bespoke version of Zodiac Aerospace's Aura seats, are fully reclining and designed for supreme comfort, converting to 180° lie-flat beds. Greenpoint increased the widths of each seat and arranged the seating area in a staggered 2x2x2 configuration to provide extra-wide aisleways, accommodating guests traveling in pairs. Each seat reclined to a full lie-flat configuration of 70.5 inches, and featured

BELOW • *Spectacular open-air seating area affords passengers unrivalled views of an airport and its surroundings.* LUFTHANSA TECHNIK

RIGHT • *The all-new Explorer design features the first and strictly limited BRABUS motorcycle, the BRABUS 1300 R, created in collaboration with leading Austrian motorcycle manufacturer KTM.* LUFTHANSA TECHIK

customised privacy surrounds, a four-way adjustable headrest and individual storage ottoman.

An executive chef prepared cuisine, in two state-of-the-art galleys.

At the time of writing, the future of Crystal Skye is uncertain, following the suspension of Crystal Cruises as a result of parent Genting Hong Kong's insolvency. The company previously sold its Boeing 787-8 for $25m to Resorts World Las Vegas, which commented: "As the only resort-owned airplane of this size in Las Vegas, this purchase opens up new opportunities for the resort's potential and existing luxury customers, as well as large groups and premium mass segments seeking easy and exclusive travel options, offering an amenity not currently available in the marketplace."

Airbus Corporate Jets

More than 210 Airbus corporate jets are in service worldwide, flying on every continent, including Antarctica.

In addition to its narrowbody product line based on the A320 family and soon to be introduced ACJ TwoTwenty, which will start operations with launch customer Comlux early 2023, ACJ widebodies are based on the A330, A340, A350 and A380 aircraft.

The ACJ350-900 XWB can fly 25 passengers 11,100nm (20,550km) or for more than 22 hours in its ultra-long range version. The Xtra wide cabin, which is six inches wider than its closest competitor, provides 270m^2 (2,905sq ft) of space on the ACJ350-900 and 308m^2 (3,315sq ft) of cabin space on the ACJ350-1000 variant. Both offer up to eight temperature zones and a hospital grade filtration system.

"The ACJ350 XWB is the ultimate in modern, long-haul, private jet travel, with the capability to deliver large groups nonstop to the world in unmatched comfort, efficiency and reliability," says ACJ president Benoit Defforge. The A350 XWB is the first Airbus aircraft to feature a carbon fibre fuselage and wings and its technological features also include the greater comfort of a lower cabin-altitude, simpler and faster transition-training for pilots through the newest version of Airbus's common cockpit, and aerodynamically efficient wings that adapt their shape in flight.

Cabin outfitting can be facilitated by ACJ's Easyfit design concept, which features preinstalled attachments and standardised interfaces that greatly simplify installing walls and furniture in a carbon fibre fuselage. A pre-engineered concept developed with cabin outfitter AMAC Aerospace, Jet Aviation and Lufthansa Technik, the Easyfit package also contains specific avionics for VIP cabin systems.

In 2019, The German government became the first state customer of the aircraft, when it placed an order for three ACJ350- 900 XWBs, destined for a mix of government, troop transport and medical evacuation roles. The first of them was delivered in 2020, with the other two planned for 2022.

BELOW • *The Orbis Flying Eye Hospital provides life changing sight operations around the world, thanks to the generosity of an army of supporters.* ORBIS

LEFT • *The German government's ACJ350XWB 'Air Force One'.* AIRBUS - STEFAN KRUIJER

Creative canvas

Introduced in 2017, the ACJ330 neo Family can fly 25 passengers for up to 22 hours nonstop up to a range of 10,400nm (19,300km), and boasts new-generation engines and Sharklets.

As a classic widebody aircraft, it offers sufficient space for a large number of new cabin ideas. Four approved cabin outfitters (AMAC Aerospace, Comlux, Jet Aviation and Lufthansa Technik), offer the cabin design concept, Harmony, which builds on the Airspace cabin brand from the Airbus airliner family.

"Long-haul flights provide time for productive work and socialising, as well as rest, and ACJ's Harmony cabin concept is wonderfully well designed to enable all of these, while bringing the world within a single flight," commented Benoit Defforge.

"Harmony is a timeless and elegant design concept, because we dare to break the conventions that are traditionally imposed on us as cabin designers. Our creativity needs to be unique to fit the needs of our customers, as befits a host receiving their guests in their 'world above the world'," added ACJ's head of creative design Sylvain Mariat.

A holographic globe, showing aircraft position, greets entering passengers. Turning left leads to the master bedroom, office, and bathroom, while turning right brings travellers into a spacious lounge with seating grouped at round tables that encourage social interaction.

BELOW • *Airbus expanded its corporate jet family with the new ACJ350 XWB version with Easyfit cabin provisions, which is the world's most modern VIP widebody jet.* AIRBUS

BBJ 747-8, 787-8/9, 777-8/9 technical characteristics

	BBJ 747-8	BBJ 787-8	BBJ 787-9	BBJ 777-8	BBJ 777-9
Length	76.3m (250ft 2in)	56.69m (186ft 9in)	63m (206ft)	69.8m (229ft)	76.7m (251ft 9in)
Height	19.4m (63ft 6in)	16.92m (55ft 6in)	17m (55ft 10in)	19.5m (64ft)	19.5m (64ft)
Fuselage width	6.5m (21ft 3in)	5.77m (18ft 9in)	5.77m (18ft 9in)	6.2m (20ft 3in)	6.2m (20ft 3in)
Wingspan	68.4m (224ft 5in)	60.17m (197ft 4in)	60.17m (197ft 4in)	71.8m (235ft 5in)	71.8m (235ft 5in)
Cabin length	63.2m (207. 5in)	51m (167ft 4in)	48.43m (206ft 7in)	N/A	48.4m (158ft 9in)
Max cabin width	6.1m (20ft 1in)	5.49m (18ft)	5.49m (18ft)	6m (19ft 7in)	5.96m (19ft 5in)
Cabin floor area	444.6m^2 (4,768sq ft)	224.4m^2 (2,415sq ft)	257.8m^2 (2,775sq ft)	302.5m^2 (3,256sq ft)	342.7m^2 (3,688sq ft)
Max take-off weight	447 tonnes (987,000lb)	172 tonnes (379,996lb)	254 tonnes (560,000lb)	351 tonnes (775,000lb)	249 tonnes (550,300 lb)
Max landing weight	312 tonnes (688,000lb)	172 tonnes (380,000lb)	193 tonnes (425,000lb)	253 tonnes (557,000lb)	192 tonnes (425,500lb)
Max zero fuel weight	243 tonnes (536,100lb)	161 tonnes (355,000lb)	181 tonnes (400,000lb)	239 tonnes (527,000lb)	N/A
Max fuel capacity	238,595 lit (63,030 US gal)	126,205 lit (33,340 US gal)	126,429 lit (33,399 US gal)	197,977 lit (52,300 US gal)	197,976 lit (52,300 US gal)
Engine	4x General Electric GEnx 2B67 Turbofan (4 x 66,500lbf)	4x Rolls-Royce Trent 1000 or General Electric GEnx-1B Turbofan (4 x 64,000lbf)	2x GEnx-1B or Rolls-Royce Trent 1000 Turbofan (2 x 71,000lbf)	2x General Electric GE9X Turbofan (2 x 105,000lbf)	2x General Electric GE9X Turbofan (2 x 105,000lbf)
Typical cruise speed	M.085	M.077	M.073	M.077	M.077
Max flight level	43,000ft	43,000ft	43,100ft	43,100ft	43,100ft

Source: Boeing

RIGHT • *Airbus A350 VIP 'Welcome Home' interior concept from Lufthansa Technik.* LUFTHANSA TECHNIK

RIGHT • *The interior of Royal Jet's BBJ737-700.* JAN BRANDES/ BY COURTESY OF ROYAL JET/LUFTHANSA TECHNIK AG

Concentric circles, like ripples on a pond, are a feature of the cabin layout. Just beyond the lounge is a conference table, and beyond that there are four VIP guest suites – each featuring an office that converts to a bedroom including an ensuite bathroom with shower.

Seating for support staff and a galley make up the rear of the cabin, which can be adapted to serve both private and government customers.

In 2014, Airbus had launched a new VIP cabin concept, initially for the A330-200.

'Summit' featured a VIP section at the front of the cabin, and airline-style seating at the rear, offering a faster and more affordable way to the greater capacity, capability, and comfort of a widebody for both private and government customers.

The Airbus ACJ330 Summit features a bedroom with ensuite bathroom at the front, followed by an office, a conference and dining room and a working area, and then airline-style first-class and economy seating at the rear.

Explorer

At the Monaco Yacht Show 2021, Lufthansa Technik previewed a new cabin design study for long-haul aircraft, for a completely new target group, with further design elements revealed at that year's Dubai Airshow. 'Explorer' is based on the current trend for superyachts of the same name.

According to Wieland Timm, head of sales for VIP & Special Mission Aircraft Services at Lufthansa Technik: "For this fast-growing target group of VIP world explorers, we have therefore now created a flying platform for the first time. Unlike a yacht, however, our Explorer aircraft allows passengers to travel to the other side of the globe within hours and set up their own individual base camp for further activities. This opens up completely new possibilities for explorers."

Paying attention to multifunctional solutions and the widest possible range of uses is the adaptable room in the rear of the aircraft, which can be used for fitness and wellness facilities on long-haul flights, or during emergencies, can be converted into a flying hospital room.

These ideas are designed for 10-16 passengers and explicitly focus on achieving the best passenger experience possible. Further modular variants for up to 47 passengers are also possible using the concept. These can include, for example, a much more individual owner's module with a master bedroom and bathroom as well as an office, but also larger areas for the crew or additional entourage.

A striking feature is a large-scale integrated projection system for virtual content, which extends from the window belt to almost the entire cabin ceiling in the multifunctional lounge area. Small, lightweight, and passively cooled projectors from Diehl, are positioned into the sidewall and ceiling elements, to create large-scale virtual impressions depending on the projection content used, such as an underwater world, sky theme, disco or architectural.

"We created a unique interior to exploit the full potential of the projection system for private jets. The overall look of a VIP cabin can be changed by a fingertip," commented Michael Bork, aircraft interior architect with the VIP & Special Mission Aircraft Service.

A unique feature is the proposed open-air seating area, a floor in the forward fuselage area, which extends outward from the parked aircraft to form a spacious veranda. The main deck cargo hatch, which is available ex works from the A330 freighter, which is now also available as a retrofit solution for passenger versions, opens up the Explore interior to its surroundings, into which passengers can then immerse themselves directly via a platform that can be extended by several metres.

It is also proposed to create a special mobility lounge in the aft section of the lower deck, which can already be viewed from the main deck through a glass floor. The area will be created in cooperation with BRABUS, a leading manufacturer of high-performance and luxury automobiles. Via a staircase, the Luxury Mobility Lounge will be easily accessible to passengers from the main deck, even during the flight, and will also cater to the technical needs of any automotives carried on board.

ABOVE • *Through BBJ Select, BBJ customers can customise the cabin interiors of the BBJ 737-7 with a wide range of pre-designed cabin layouts and configurations.*
BOEING

BELOW LEFT • *A Boeing 787 VIP interior concept.*
BOEING

BELOW RIGHT • *A Boeing 747-8 concept interior.*
BOEING

ABOVE LEFT • *Boeing Business Jets delivers the airplanes to customers unpainted and without an interior. A completion centre of the customer's choosing installs the jet's VIP interior.* BOEING

ABOVE RIGHT • *Boeing's first Aeroloft installation on a BBJ 747-8.* BOEING

BELOW • *The government of Poland uses two new BBJ 2 airplanes and one 737-800 as head-of-state aircraft for the president and top government officials.* BOEING

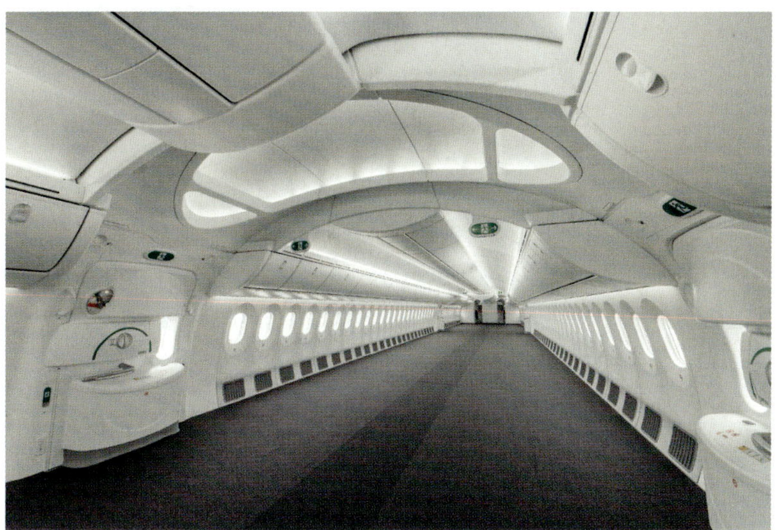

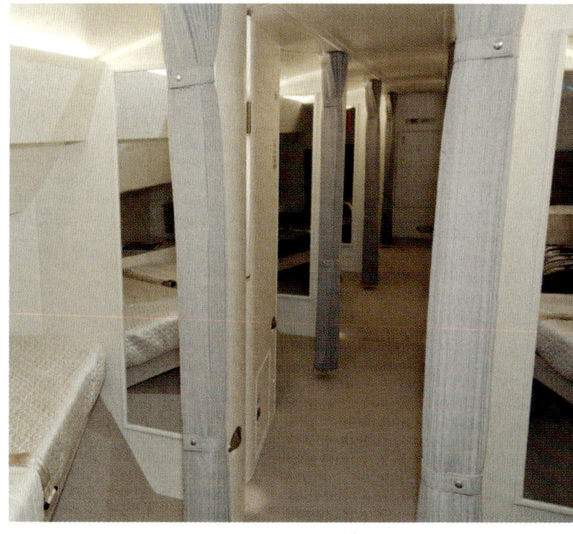

Flying eye

Away from the glitz and glamour of a private aircraft, one special widebody is delivering a very functional and life changing service.

In 2016, Orbis, the global non-governmental organisation (NGO) launched the third generation Orbis Flying Eye Hospital. A former cargo plane, the MD-10 (a McDonnell Douglas DC-10-30, retrofitted with the MD-10-30 upgrade) was donated by long-time sponsor FedEx in 2012.

The Flying Eye Hospital is the world's only airplane with a fully functioning state-of-the-art eye hospital on board using a modular design concept. MMIC (Mobile Medical International Corporation) designed and manufactured the modules, which are a first for an aircraft.

This third incarnation of the Flying Eye Hospital can fly nearly twice as far as its predecessor, which was donated to the Pima Air and Space Museum in Tucson, Arizona and requires only two pilots rather than three.

The conversion took more than six years to complete, with hundreds of experts, including the FedEx aircraft maintenance team, contribute their avionics, hospital engineering, technology, and clinical expertise.

The plane includes a 46-seat classroom, with 3D technology allowing filming and broadcast from the operating room for students to view in the adjacent classroom as well as in other classrooms outside of the aircraft. Simulations may also be conducted, and participants may pose questions via two-way video and audio.

Other features include sterilisation and laser rooms.

The COVID-19 pandemic grounded the Flying Eye Hospital, but instead of being put into storage, the aircraft was kept in a constant state of flight readiness at Alliance International Airport in Fort Worth, Texas.

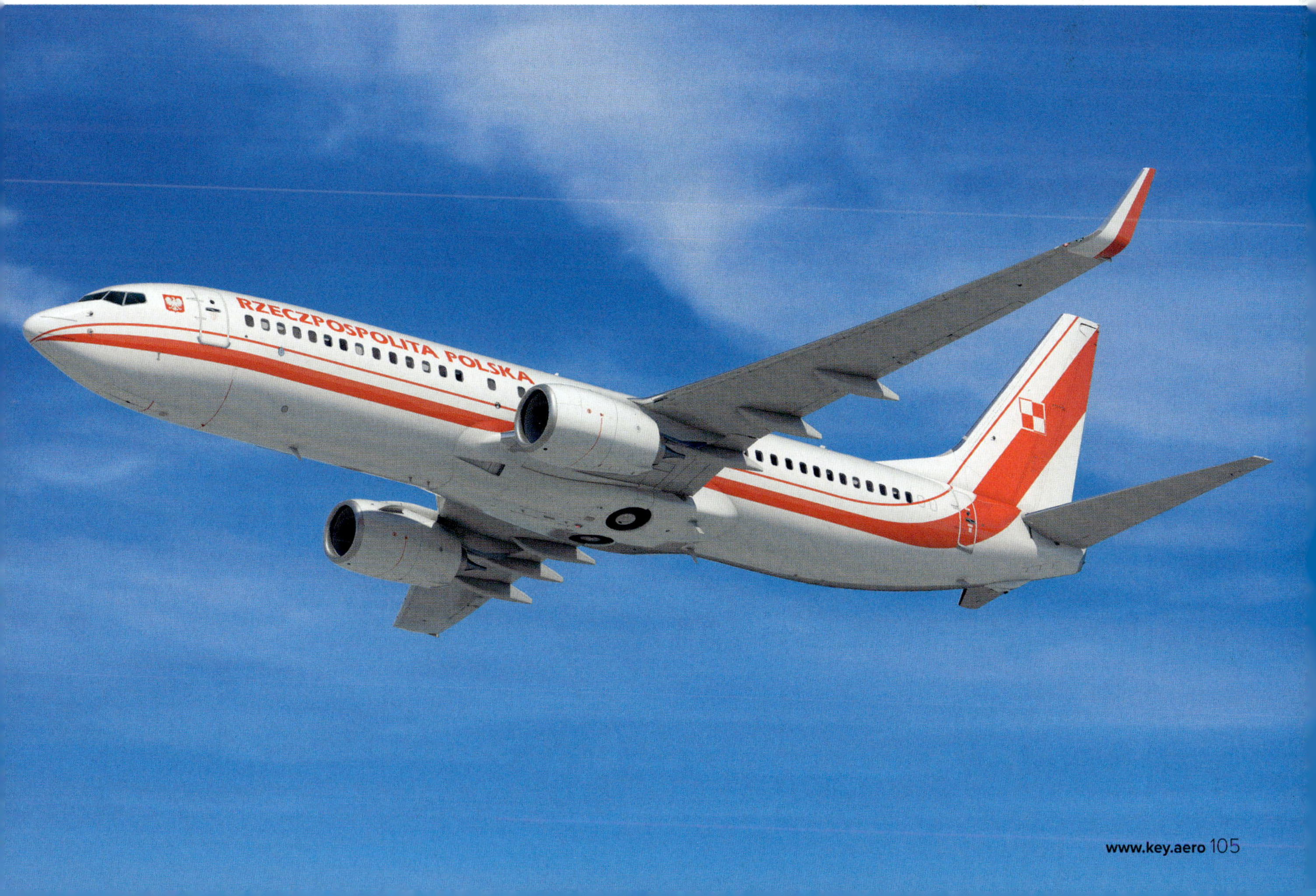

RIGHT • *In March 2022, Emirates, the largest customer of the world's largest commercial jet marked the end of its 21-year commitment to the A380 programme with delivery of A6 EVS to its fleet.* EMIRATES

The Path Ahead

A new generation of more efficient, sustainable widebodies is reinvigorating the twin-aisle market with new levels of comfort, ensuring the viability of these behemoths for many years to come.

The COVID-19 pandemic may have receded, but the challenges it has posed look set to remain for some time. It's unsurprising that demand for domestic air travel lead the industry's recovery. As health and travel restrictions eased, we a pick-up in intra-regional markets but for long-haul it was a different story. Here took a little longer to return to pre-pandemic levels, with demand only surpassing pre-pandemic levels in 2024.

According to Boeing's Commercial Market Outlook 2024-2043, single aisle airplanes comprise nearly 66% of today's global passenger jet fleet. In the next 20 years, this share will increase to over 71%, or 35,835 passenger airplanes.

This growth is being partly driven by the renaissance of long-range narrowbody aircraft, namely the A220-300, Boeing 737MAX, A321LR and A321XLR with their respective capabilities to fly from 6,300km up to 8,700km.

Past performance

During the 1960s, narrowbodies were commonly used for transatlantic flights: the Boeing 707-320B had the capacity to fly routes up to 10,000km. But as widebodies emerged, the use of narrowbodies on long-haul routes fell out of favour. Until now.

As Valour Consultancy point out, there is evidence to suggests a new hybrid market is opening up, which will offer passengers a 'widebody-lite' onboard environment. In other words, a widebody cabin experience on a narrowbody aircraft.

For example, towards the end of 2021, Singapore Airlines rolled out a S$230m (£136m) investment in new cabin products (seating, inflight entertainment, and connectivity) across its new fleet of Boeing 737-8 aircraft, which will used on short-medium haul routes. In doing so, the carrier is replicating the onboard experience with that of its widebody fleet.

While Airbus had to wait until June to receive its first widebody order of 2021 (An A350 from Lufthansa)

the future for widebodies is still bright, if not a little luminous.

Of the 50,170 aircraft projected to be in operation by 2043, Boeing foresees 8,750 to be widebody, occupying a stable 17% market share. In its estimates, Airbus sees similar numbers, with 21% of all new deliveries being widebodies. Of the 8,820 widebody aircraft it believes will be delivered by 2043, the overwhelming majority are destined for the Middle East.

But one aircraft model that won't be among those delivered is the A380.

The demise of a giant

In early 2019, Emirates, the world's largest operator of A380s, took the decision to reduce its A380 orderbook from 162 to 123 aircraft, citing a review of its operations and advances in aircraft and engine technologies

Commenting on the decision, Airbus' chief executive officer Tom Enders said: "As a result of this decision we have no substantial A380 backlog and hence no basis to

ABOVE • *A380 MSN1 has helped play a significant role in steps to achieve certification of 100% SAF by 2030.* AIRBUS SAS 2022 ALEXANDRE DOUMENJOU - MASTER FILMS

LEFT • *Following a three-year development phase, Singapore Airlines has enhanced its narrowbody cabin experience to a level similar to that found on its widebody fleet.* SINGAPORE AIRLINES

ABOVE • *Unveiled in 2022, the ZEROe demonstrator uses an A380 multimodal platform to evaluate hydrogen combustion technology.* AIRBUS

BELOW • *Designed by long-time collaborator David Caon, the six first class suites on Qantas' forthcoming A350 aircraft will set new standards in premium travel.* ARTIST RENDER - QANTAS

sustain production, despite all our sales efforts with other airlines in recent years. This leads to the end of A380 deliveries in 2021."

He added that: "The A380 is not only an outstanding engineering and industrial achievement. Passengers all over the world love to fly on this great aircraft. Hence today's announcement is painful for us and the A380 communities worldwide. But keep in mind that A380s will still roam the skies for many years to come and Airbus will of course continue to fully support the A380 operators."

Ten airlines, including Emirates, continue to operate the A380. In December 2021, Emirates received delivery of its 123rd and final Airbus A380, six months ahead of the original delivery date.

Sir Tim Clark, president of Emirates Airline said of the occasion: "The A380 is a truly special aircraft in so many ways. For Emirates, it gave us the opportunity to redefine the travel experience, efficiently serve demand at slot-constrained airports, and bolster our network growth. The A380 will remain Emirates' flagship product for the coming years, and a vital pillar of our network plans."

A fresh start

While it may have ceased as a production aircraft, one A380 has been given a second life as a test aircraft. In March 2022, Airbus' A380 test aircraft MSN 1, the first-ever A380 to roll off the production line, took off from Blagnac Airport, Toulouse, France for a three-hour flight operating one Rolls-Royce Trent 900 engine on 100% sustainable aviation fuel (SAF). The aircraft made a second flight at the end of the month, to evaluate the use of SAF during take-off and landing, increasing engine exposure to 100% SAF.

While the first flight test phase focused on outboard engine behaviour of 100% SAF and APU (auxiliary power unit) testing, the second flight test phase tested this fuel type on the inboard engine and its impact on fuel gauging.

"Due to the A380's engine and fuel system configuration, analysing engine and fuel system behaviours with 100% SAF needs to be managed over multiple flights," stated François Pfindel, Airbus' head of A380 MAP. "In doing so, we'll generate a wealth of data that will help us to complement the research programmes currently underway."

"This is the first time that unblended SAF has been used on an A380 flight test platform," explained Airbus test pilot Wolfgang Absmeier. "The flight test met all of our requirements, which will enable us to carry out the next phase of the project consisting of specific engine manoeuvres."

The A380 is the third Airbus aircraft type to fly on 100% SAF over the course of 12 months; the first was an Airbus A350 (Volcan) in March 2021 followed by an A319neo single-aisle aircraft (ECLIF3) in October 2021.

All Airbus aircraft are currently certified to fly with up to a 50% blend of SAF mixed with kerosene. The aim is to achieve certification of 100% SAF by the end of this decade.

The flight test campaign is supported by a variety of partners. Rolls-Royce conducted compatibility studies related to the engine adaptation for the Trent 900. Pratt & Whitney is providing support for the APU. TotalEnergies supplied the unblended SAF.

"This is another great example of the aviation industry coming together to work towards achieving certification of

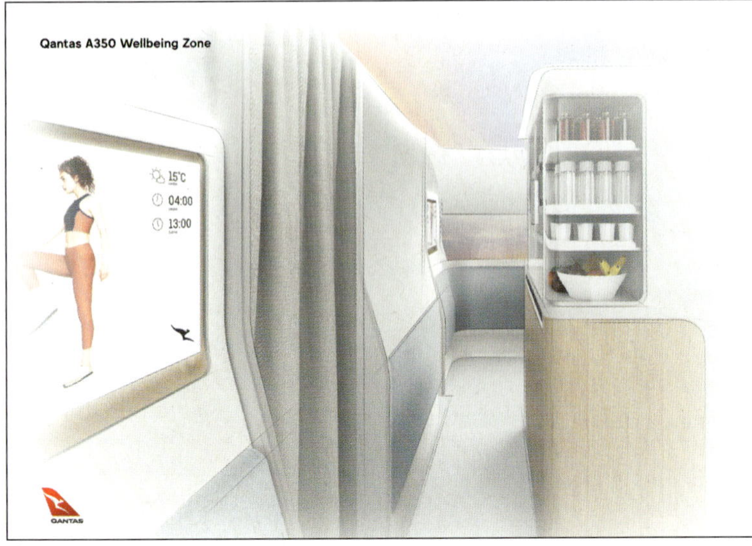

ABOVE • Qantas A350 passengers can stretch their legs in the new Wellbeing Zone, complete with a self-serve snack station and digital displays providing movement and stretching recommendations.
ARTIST RENDER - QANTAS

BELOW • Boeing's 777-9 flight test plane touched down at Dubai's Airshow in late 2021, on its first international flight.
BOEING

100% SAF by 2030," stated Pfindel. "Together, we've clearly demonstrated that an aircraft as large as the A380 can successfully operate on unblended SAF."

With the test campaign over, the A380 MSN1 will be renovated to restore its aircraft testing capability and subsequently transformed into the ZEROe demonstrator to test hydrogen combustion technology in years to come.

Test bed

ZEROe is Airbus' multi-year demonstrator programme to assess a variety of hydrogen technologies both on the ground and in the air and is part of Airbus' ambition to develop the world's first zero-emission commercial aircraft by 2035.

"The A380 MSN1 is an excellent flight laboratory platform for new hydrogen technologies," believes Mathias Andriamisaina, Airbus ZEROe demonstrator leader. "It's a safe and reliable platform that is highly versatile to test a wide range of zero-emission technologies. In addition, the platform can comfortably accommodate the large flight test instrumentation that will be needed to analyse the performance of the hydrogen in the hydrogen-propulsion system."

CFM International, a joint venture between GE and Safran, will develop the hydrogen combustion engine and prepare it for testing. The engine in question is a GE Passport turbofan which will undergo a modification of its combustor, fuel system and control system to run on hydrogen. The engine was selected due to its physical size, advanced turbo machinery, and fuel flow capability.

The hydrogen tanks, hydrogen combustion engine and liquid hydrogen distribution system will be assessed individually on the ground. The complete system will then be evaluated first on the ground and then subsequently in flight, which is expected to take place in the next five years.

Back in 2015, A380 MSN1 tested one of the most powerful engines ever developed for an Airbus aircraft. Designed for the A350-1000 aircraft, the performance of the engine under a wide range of power settings at altitudes of up to 35,000ft were assessed during a four-hour 14-minute flight.

Boeing ecoDemonstrator

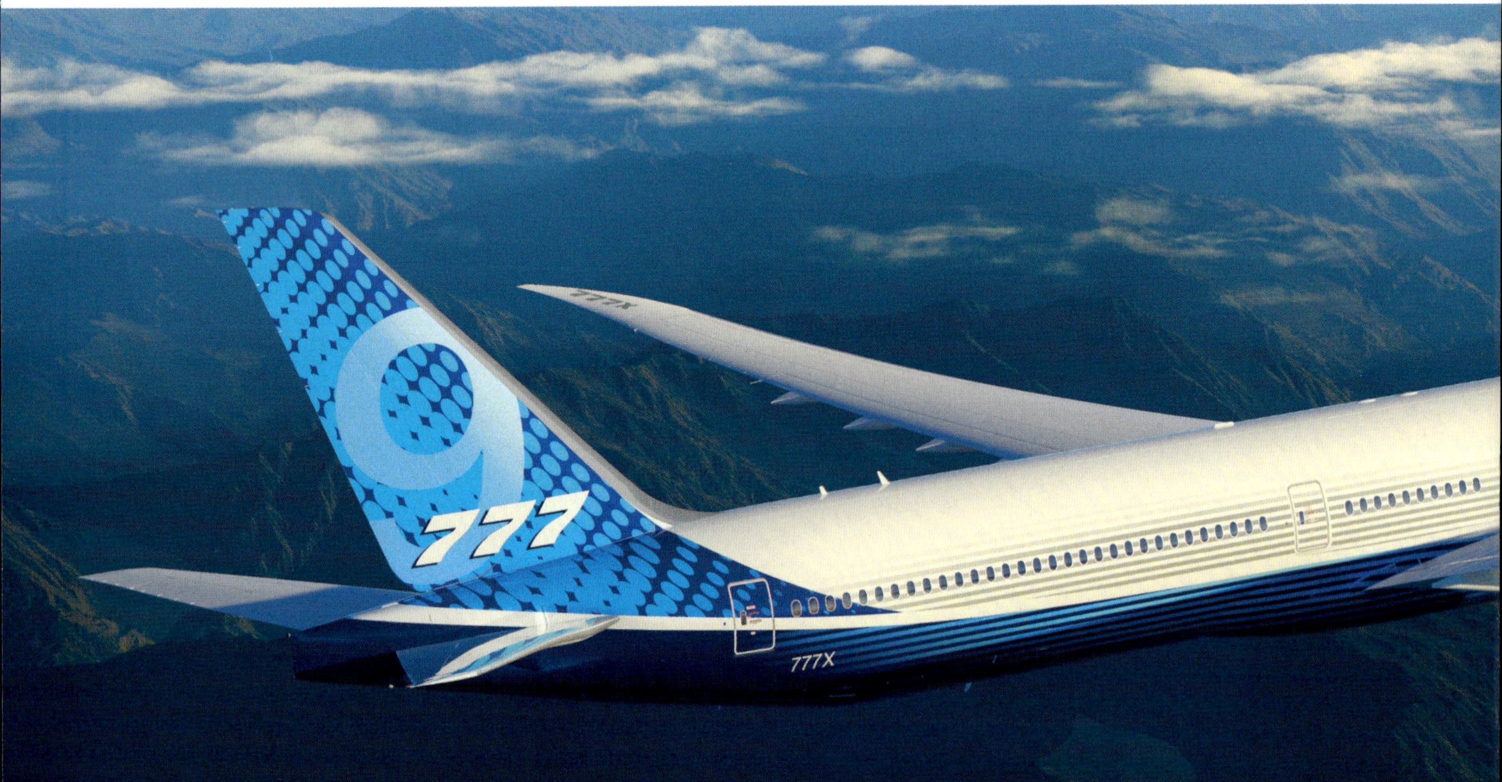

Boeing meanwhile has fulfilled the first ten of 30 technology evaluations on its latest ecoDemonstrator that sports a

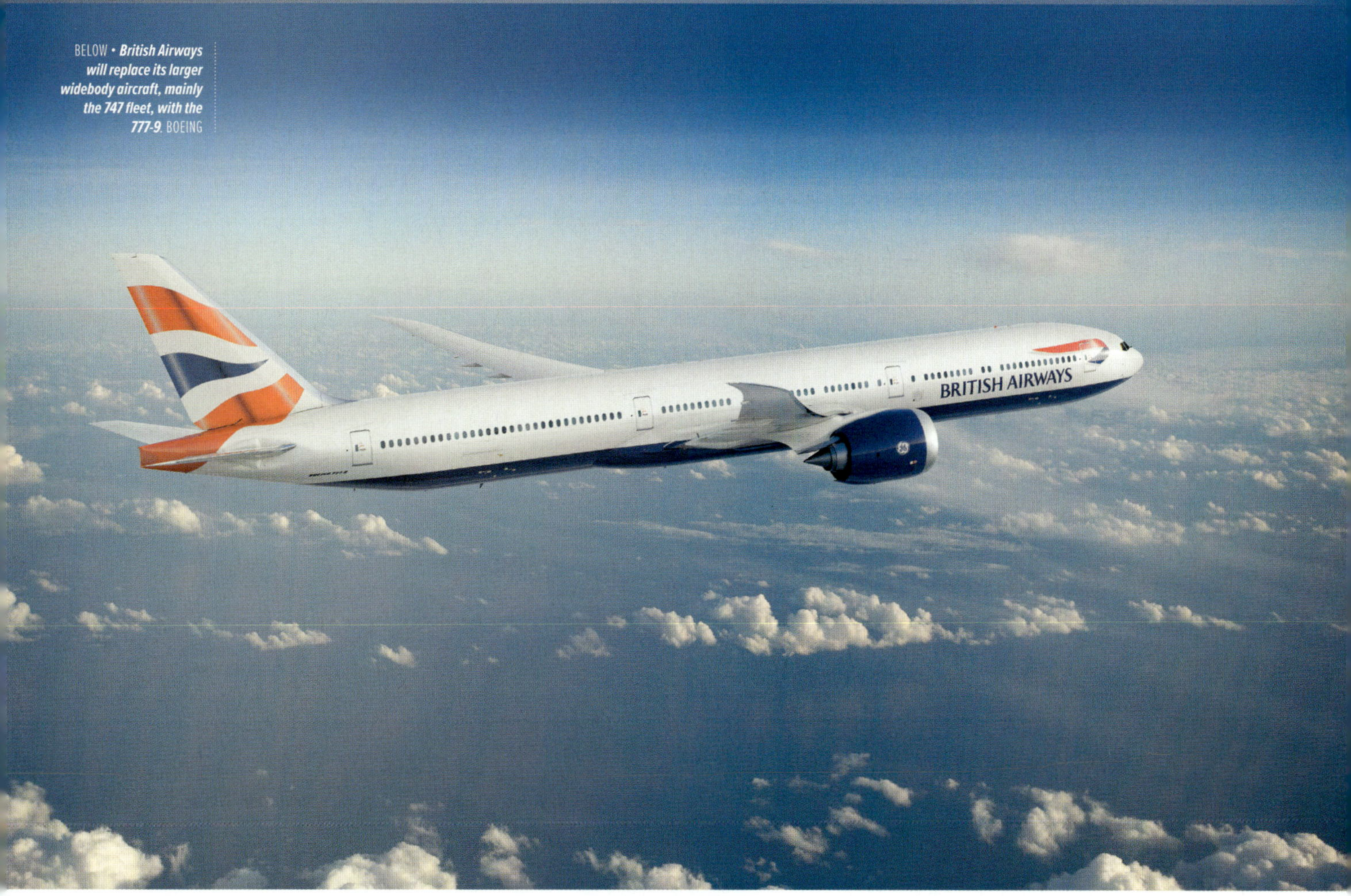

BELOW • ***British Airways will replace its larger widebody aircraft, mainly the 747 fleet, with the 777-9.*** BOEING

livery that honours a decade of testing to reduce fuel use, emissions, and noise.

The current ecoDemonstrator is a Boeing-owned 777-200ER, which will test 30 new technologies aimed at improving sustainability and safety for the aerospace industry, including a water conservation system and technologies to improve operational efficiency.

"The Boeing ecoDemonstrator program helps us make tangible improvements to our products – allowing us to reduce the environmental impacts of flying, improve the in-flight experience and strengthen the safety of our airplanes," said Stephanie Pope, president and CEO of Boeing Commercial Airplanes. "We're grateful for the many partnerships within aviation and beyond who help us turn the seemingly impossible into reality."

"The ecoDemonstrator program is among our most iconic flight demonstrators, having tested 250 technologies since it first took flight in 2012," said Brian Moran, Boeing Chief Sustainability Officer.

For all flight tests, the 777-200ER flies on the highest approved blend of sustainable aviation fuel (SAF) available..

"The Boeing ecoDemonstrator programme brings together the two most important ingredients to a more sustainable future – innovative technologies and partnerships with customers, suppliers, government agencies and academia," said Chris Raymond, Boeing's chief sustainability officer. "We celebrate the past successes and look forward to continuing this iconic program to help decarbonize aviation, together."

Since its initial flights in 2012, the Boeing ecoDemonstrator programme has accelerated innovation by taking new technologies out of the lab and testing them in an operational environment. Including this year's platform, the

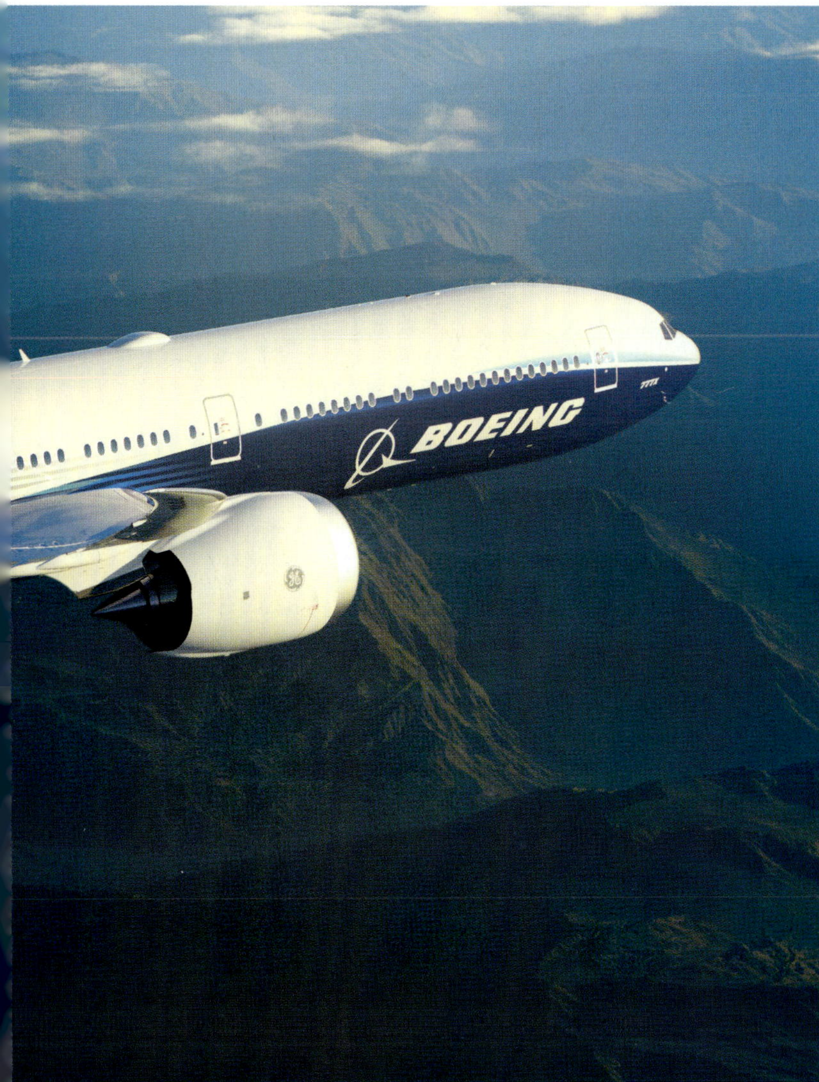

programme has evaluated about 230 technologies to help decarbonise aviation, improve operational efficiency and enhance safety and the passenger experience. Approximately a third of tested technologies have progressed onto Boeing's products and services.

A new dawn

Despite the decision of Emirates to forego any new A380 deliveries, the Middle Eastern airline is putting its faith in Airbus' newest generation, flexible widebody aircraft, the A350-900.

For Qantas Group CEO Alan Joyce, "New types of aircraft make new things possible." During a ceremony in Sydney attended by Joyce and Airbus' chief commercial officer and head of Airbus International, Christian Scherer, in May 2022, he announced a commitment for 12 Airbus A350-1000 aircraft – the selected model for Project Sunrise with flights scheduled for late 2027, initially from Sydney to London.

"The A350 and Project Sunrise will make any city just one flight away from Australia. It's the last frontier and the final fix for the tyranny of distance," he said.

In 2017, Qantas challenged Boeing and Airbus to deliver an aircraft capable of ultra-long-haul flying, enabling non-stop flights to Australia from any other city including New York, London, Paris, and Frankfurt. Codenamed Project Sunrise in honour of the Double Sunrise flights operated by Qantas across the Indian Ocean during World War Two which remained airborne long enough to see two sunrises, the initiative began in earnest in 2019 with three research flights over three months using brand new Boeing 787-9s.

The aircraft simulated two Project Sunrise routes – London and New York to Sydney taking around 19 hours each, subject to wind and weather conditions, with a maximum 40 people, including crew, onboard aircraft, to gather data about inflight passenger and crew health and wellbeing.

Collaborating with scientists and medical experts from the Sydney-based Charles Perkins Centre, those in the cabin (predominantly Qantas employees) were fitted with wearable technology devices to monitor sleep patterns, food and beverage consumption, lighting, physical movement, and inflight entertainment to assess impact on health, wellbeing, and body clock, at varying stages of the flights.

Pilots also took part in the research, with Monash University, Melbourne researchers recording crew melatonin levels before, during and after the flights. Pilots wore an EEG

ABOVE • *A Qantas A350-1000 arrives at Sydney Airport as part of the A350 Australian demo tour.* AIRBUS SAS 2022 - QANTAS JAMES D. MORGAN

(electroencephalogram) device that tracks brain wave patterns and monitors alertness as part of efforts to understand and establish data in building the optimum work and rest pattern for pilots operating long haul services. Qantas gained almost 60 hours of Project Sunrise flying experience across the three flights and thousands of data points which helped shape the cabin design.

Powered by Rolls-Royce Trent XWB-97 turbofan engines which are 25% more fuel efficient than previous generation aircraft, the A350-100 will have the capacity to carry 238 passengers, the lowest of any A350-1000 currently in service, across four classes (first, business, premium economy, and economy), with more than 40% of the cabin dedicated to premium seating.

All in the details

Working with long-term Airbus and Qantas collaborator, the Australian industrial designer David Caon, first-class features six suites in a two-row 1-1-1 configuration, complete with privacy door, separate bed and Ottoman lounge chair for comfort or productivity. Entertainment comes via an impressive 32in inflight entertainment screen and while there are no overhead lockers, there is ample storage courtesy of a personal wardrobe built into the wall panelling, a large fold-out storage bin suitable for a backpack or laptop bag below the monitor, and a shoe drawer concealed within the Ottoman.

BELOW • *The Boeing 2022 ecoDemonstrator (777-200ER) will assess 30 technologies to enhance safety and sustainability.* BOEING

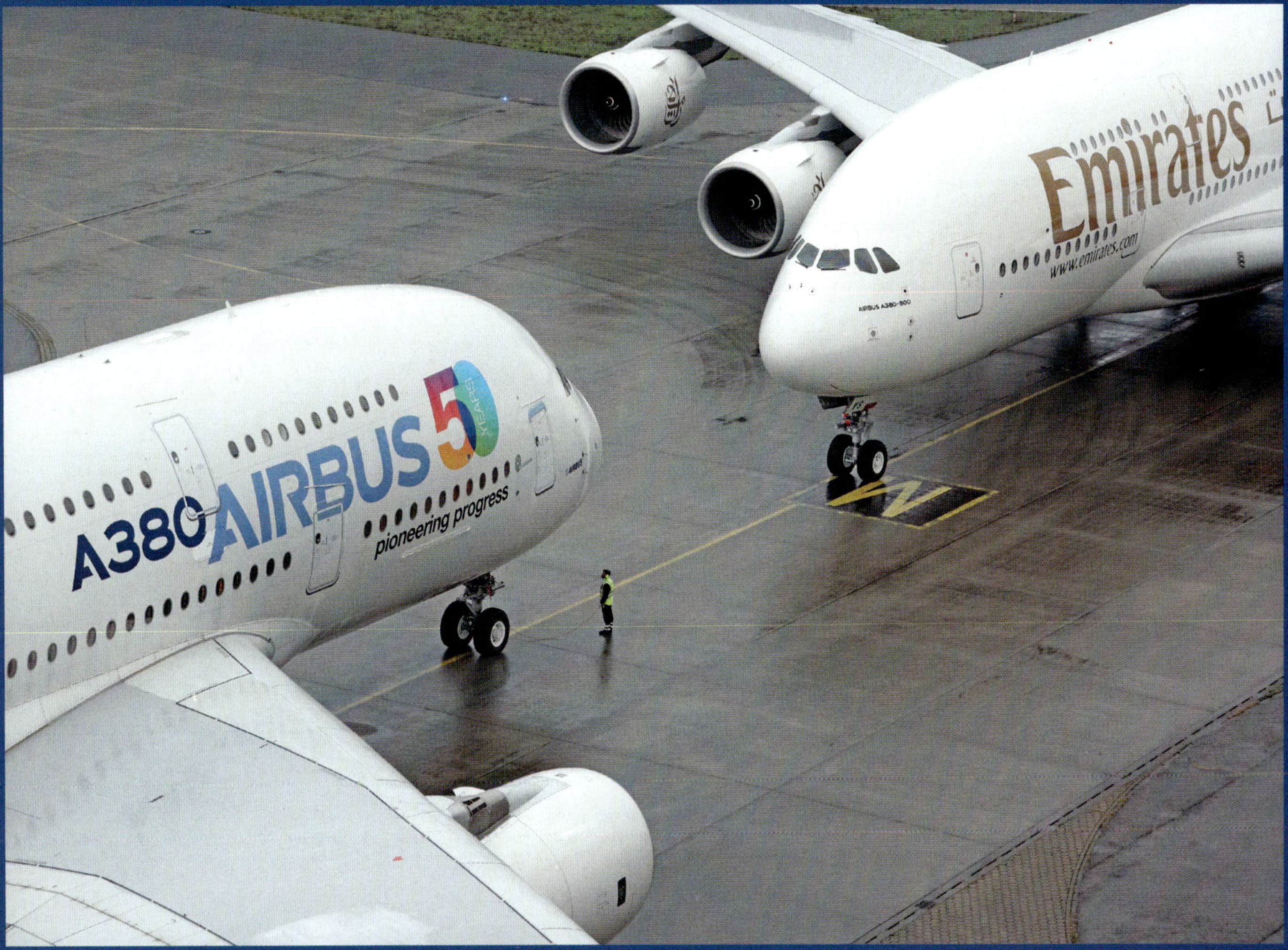

ABOVE • *Nose to nose. A380 Airbus MSN001 and A380 Emirates MSN272 together.* AIRBUS-LUTZ BORCK

BELOW • *The A380 is the largest passenger aircraft ever built - ideal for use as a flight test platform to mature hydrogen combustion technology.* AIRBUS

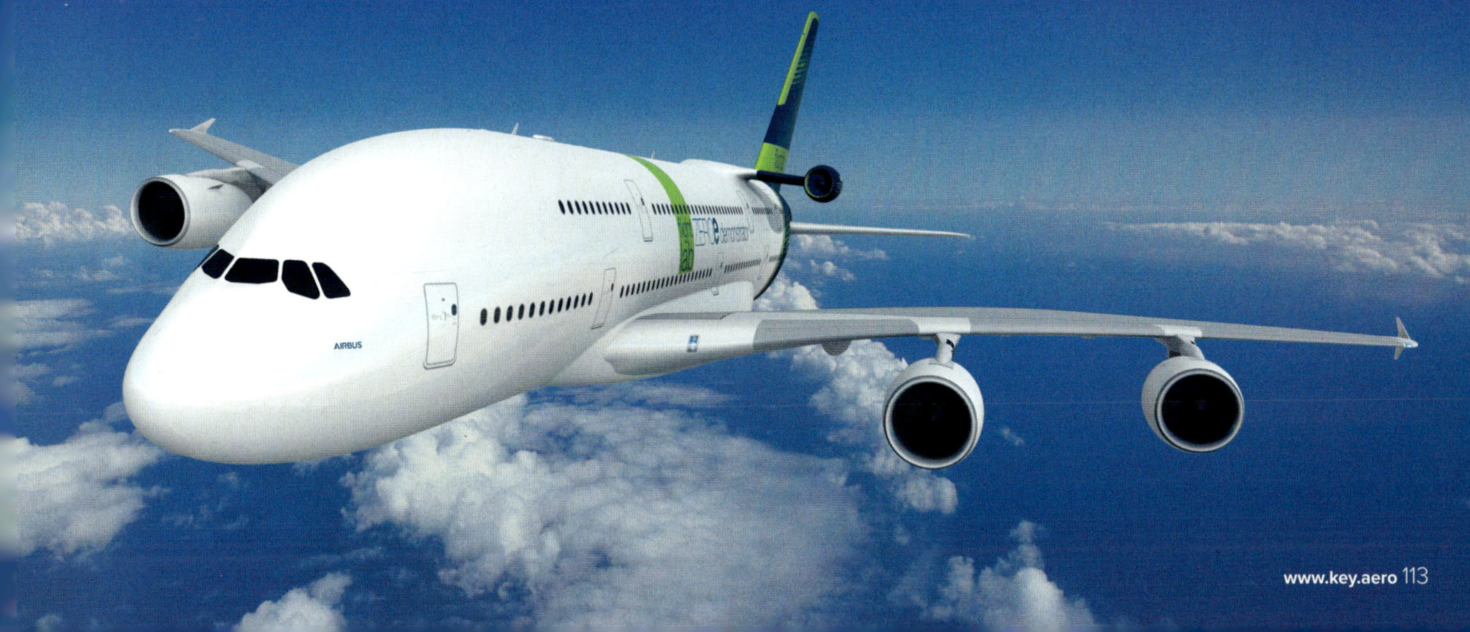

There is an integrated shelving unit next to the IFE screen for amenity kits as well as a mirror on the inside. An iPad gives the passenger personal control over the suite's functions and settings, including tailored lighting, temperature, and humidity for wellbeing.

The A350s will also include next-generation business-class suites, new premium economy seats at a 40in pitch, and new economy seats at a 33in pitch.

The cabin is specially configured for improved comfort on long flights and includes a wellbeing zone in the centre (between premium economy and economy), where passengers can move and stretch. Videos on digital displays provide guidance. There is also a self-service snack station.

In announcing the deal with Airbus, which included the renewal of its narrowbody jets as part of Project Winton (with firm orders for 20 Airbus A321XLRs and 20 A220-300s to replace its retired Boeing 737s and 717s), Joyce said: "For more than 100 years, Qantas has been at the forefront of transforming the way the world travels, particularly through direct flights.

"Our direct Perth-London flights started in 2017 and showed strong demand for the convenience and time savings from this kind of travel if the product and service is right. Pre-COVID it was the longest route on our network and had the highest customer satisfaction on our network. All signs point to that demand increasing post-COVID.

"The Qantas A350 travel experience will be truly exceptional, particularly across the premium cabins. Our first and business-class seats will set a new benchmark for premium long-haul travel."

On pause

In mid-October 2024 Boeing readjusted its estimates regarding timing of 777X entry into service and market demand, anticipating that the first 777X delivery would occur in 2026. In a message to employees, President and CEO Kelly Ortberg shared that, "On the 777X program, the challenges we have faced in development, as well as from the flight test pause and ongoing work stoppage, will delay our program timeline. We have notified customers that we now expect first delivery in 2026."

Patience is certainly the name of the game, as the 777X programme was launched far back at the 2013 Dubai Airshow, amidst great fanfare.

The 777X programme has been beset with multiple issues, including delays to flight tests, which resumed in January 2025 following a pause due to problems with a thrust link after a test flight in Hawaii. Ortberg has repeatedly confirmed his belief that FAA type certification will be obtained by the end of 2025 or early 2026.

Building on the best of the industry-leading 777 and 787 Dreamliner families, the 777-9 will be the world's largest and most efficient twin-engine jet, delivering 10% better fuel use, emissions, and operating costs than the competition and an exceptional passenger experience. The 777X family has a total of 250+ orders and commitments from leading customers around the globe.

In 2021, the 777X made an appearance at the Dubai Airshow. Boeing left the event with agreements four customers across Europe and the Middle East: Lufthansa); Etihad Airways ; Qatar Airways and Emirates. The combined value of the agreements was more than US$95bn at 2013 list prices - the largest product launch in commercial jetliner history by dollar value.

The launch customer for the 777-9, the first and largest variant of the 777X family, will be Lufthansa, which has ordered 20 aircraft. Driven by a post-merger transformation with Asiana Airlines, Korean Air has, at the time of writing, become the latest 777X customer, placing an order for 20 777-9s.

The 777 may be the backbone of many fleets, but these customers and potential others, will be looking forward with bated breath, to building upon their legacy with the next-generation 777-9.

ABOVE • *The 2020 ecoDemonstrator programme was the first to use a Boeing 787-10. The testing programme lasted about four weeks before the Etihad Boeing 787-10 entered into service.* BOEING

BELOW • *The 2018 ecoDemonstrator was a collaboration between Boeing and FedEx. The 777 Freighter was used to evaluate more than 30 technologies in a flight test programme.* BOEING